# Keep
# It
# Simple,
# Stupid

**Also by Judge Judy Sheindlin**

Beauty Fades, Dumb Is Forever
Don't Pee on My Leg and Tell Me It's Raining
Win or Lose by How You Choose!

# Keep It Simple, Stupid

## You're Smarter Than You Look

### JUDGE JUDY SHEINDLIN

Cliff Street Books

*An Imprint of* HarperCollins*Publishers*

This book is dedicated to the wisdom
of our grandparents, in the hope that
their grandchildren will listen.

*Designed by Ruth Lee*

Illustrations copyright © 2000 by Bob Tore

ISBN 0–06–019546–0

# CONTENTS

# ACKNOWLEDGMENTS

To Catherine Whitney, whose wit, wisdom, and organization kept me focused.

To Jane Dystel, who keeps insisting, "There's another book in you."

To Diane Reverand, my editor and friend, who gave subtle and perfect guidance.

To Bob Tore, whose illustrations added a picture of humor and pathos.

To Janet Dery, whose perseverance kept the book on track.

# INTRODUCTION:
# GOING NUCLEAR

If you've attended any weddings lately, you might have noticed that the nuclear family isn't what it used to be. The program for a modern wedding procession reads like the playbill for a Greek tragedy. Getting down the aisle requires negotiations that rival the peace talks at Versailles. The following scene is not as outlandish as it sounds.

Melvin and Sandra are getting married. Sandra's adoptive father divorced her adoptive mother, who then married her stepfather. Her birth father has recently reentered Sandra's life, so now she has three fathers vying for the right to walk her down the aisle and arguing over who should foot the bill. Sandra's adoptive mother and stepfather won't sit near Sandra's adoptive father and his fourth wife.

Melvin's children from a previous marriage are attending with his ex-in-laws, who feel they should be seated with Melvin's parents, who never could stand them. Melvin's gay brother, Billy, is the best man and is demanding that his lover be seated with the family, which offends Melvin's born-again-Christian sister and her husband. Sandra's unmarried sister, who just gave birth to a child conceived through artificial insemination, plans to nurse her baby during the ceremony.

The wedding will be officiated by a priest for Melvin, a rabbi for Sandra, a Methodist minister in deference to Sandra's adoptive father, and a judge who is married to Melvin's second cousin.

# Could World War III be far behind?

Life used to be so simple. You got married when you were twenty, stayed married for fifty years, and raised children who got married when they were twenty and gave you grandchildren. Mother's Day and Father's Day didn't look like the revolving door at Macy's. Everyone had the same religion and lived in the same neighborhood. It's not so simple anymore. Families have more to fight about. After twenty-five years in family court and four years appearing on my syndicated TV show, *Judge Judy*, I've witnessed every family crisis imaginable, from the utterly absurd to the totally serious. Convoluted family arrangements create convoluted problems. Siblings, parents, in-laws, steps, exes—the works.

Today's family has more facets than my diamond ring—and they're not half as pretty or as precious.

After all I've seen and experienced, I've come to the conclusion that people create their own unhappiness. They unnecessarily complicate their relationships by bickering over minutiae, refusing to let go of minor insults, and worrying to death about picayune matters that completely miss the big picture. If there are two ways to react to a situation, they don't ask, "What makes the most sense?" or "What would be the easiest thing to do?" They fret and fume and throw their egos around, and make themselves and everyone else miserable. I long to shout the four words of advice that would cover just about every family squabble: "Keep it simple, stupid!" Or, to put it more kindly, "K.I.S.S."

In custody disputes I heard in Family Court, otherwise sane and responsible adults would litigate *ad nauseum* about whether visitation started at six or seven o'clock Friday night, and how many pairs of socks would accompany each child.

It always struck me as a shame that they were pouring so much energy into matters that weren't important, wasting their best years on beating the dead horse of their past grievances. Lawyers would bring me settlement papers in custody and visitation cases, and you'd need a Ph.D. to figure out when Billy and Sue were being transferred back and forth:

> Every third Sunday when in baseball season the children will go with their father at 9:00. When it isn't baseball season, the children will attend church with their mother, then be picked up for soccer practice by their father at 11:00. Every third Thanksgiving the children will be with their father, provided that he is visiting his parents in San Diego. If the father is not visiting his parents, then every second Thanksgiving he can have the children at his house, provided that there is an adult female present to help bathe the little girl . . .

I kid you not. I would look at these agreements and say to myself, This is a road map for disaster. These people are going to spend the vast majority of their time trying to figure out when visitation is supposed to happen. The children will never have a routine with which they're comfortable, and children love routines.

The parents will never be able to get on with their lives, because they have bound themselves to a document that is oppressive and complicated.

Nobody does it to them. They do it to themselves. On my television program, I see people involved in relationships who have created tangled webs of complexity over finances, leases, and contracts—and they're not even committed to each other. Somebody is always left with the short end of it, and usually that person will say, "Why me?" My reply: "Why *you*? Because you did it to yourself. You allowed yourself to be put in a situation that compromised your finances. He wasn't committed enough to marry you, but you have committed yourself to paying his car loan."

There are certain themes that keep coming up again and again—the predictable conflicts that arise out of relationships:

"I want to get married, and he says it's just a piece of paper."

"We agreed not to have kids, and now she wants to get pregnant."

"I expect my husband to do his share, but he says he works hard enough."

"She thinks our son can do no wrong, but I say he needs some discipline."

"We've lived together for two years. Why can't we sleep together when we visit my folks?"

Likewise, there are themes that recur when relationships break up:

Who gets the car? Who gets the wedding silver? Who keeps the friends? When children are involved, there's a tremendous built-in opportunity for bedlam—especially when the parents insist on behaving like children themselves over custody and visitation matters.

In every disagreement, there are at least two sides. Each party is absolutely convinced of the rightness of his or her position. There's rarely an absolutely right answer. Usually, the answer lies someplace in the middle.

That's why there are judges. Someone has to decide, and it's best if it's a third party who is not emotionally involved. Throughout the book, I have developed scenarios that are composites of the many cases I've heard over the years—in Family Court, in my TV courtroom, and from people who have written to me about their problems. In each scenario, there are two sides, and sometimes three. As you read, you'll probably see yourself and people you know, because these are the ordinary problems that come up when people don't keep it simple.

# Judge Judy's Rules for Family Harmony

When people come to me with their relationship problems, they know three things right off the bat: One, I'm not their mother, and my job isn't to fix all their problems. Two, I have a built-in truth detector, so they shouldn't feed me a load of baloney. Three, they'd better keep it simple.

In the following pages, as I "rule" on a variety of family conflicts, I'll be giving my own bottom-line set of rules:

1. LIVING WITHOUT BENEFIT: If you call this commitment, you should be committed.
2. TYING THE KNOT: Ten times measure, one time cut.
3. MARRIED BLISS: If life were fair, men would have stretch marks.
4. KIDS HAPPEN: Having a baby is easy; being a parent is hard.
5. AFTER THE BALL IS OVER: Don't get mad. Get out. Move on.
6. TUG-OF-WARS: Love your kids more than you hate each other.
7. THE SECOND TIME AROUND: For better or forget about it.
8. THE FAMILY BOND: Honor your parents.
9. 'TIL DEATH DO US IN: Where there's a will, there's a way.
10. KEEP IT SIMPLE, STUPID: You're smarter than you look.

The rules, like the theme, are simple. They may seem obvious, but in the world of relationships, even what's simple and obvious can become tangled in dissent. The bottom line is, it's up to you.

# 1

# Living Without Benefit

## (If you call this commitment, you should be committed.)

In the middle-class neighborhood where I grew up, if two people lived together without benefit of marriage, they were bums and their parents were pitied. Their lives were forever on the gossipy lips of old aunts and nosy neighbors. Times have changed, and it's no longer such a scandal to do a "test run." But don't kid yourself that living together is the same as being married. If anything, it's much more complicated. There are no rules, no court of last resort when things don't work out. In my TV courtroom, I have presided over countless cases involving former live-ins. The issue usually revolves around money, possessions, and promises made and broken. It amazes me that people who turn faint at the thought of walking down the aisle think nothing of purchasing houses, boats, and cars with live-in lovers. When they try to get satisfaction from the court, they learn just why it's easier to keep things legal. I don't have a problem with two adults living together. If you choose to test the waters before jumping into the marital sea, don't kid yourself that it is a commitment until death—especially when it comes to money. So many women equate a joint bank account and credit card with commitment. Most of them are just not thinking. If a child of mine ever opened a bank account with Mr. Almost-Sort-of-Committed, I'd have *her* committed. Think how much easier it would be if we had laws for people living together. If I were to write those laws, they would include the following stipulations:

1. No live-in arrangement shall exceed one year. If after one year there is no ring on the finger or date for the wedding, the temporary partnership shall disband.
2. Live-ins shall not purchase any of the following items jointly: house, car, boat, espresso machine, dog, or health club membership.
3. All expenses shall be divided equally, and a precise record kept.
4. The word *commitment* shall be used only in referring to the upcoming wedding.

If live-ins abided by these rules, they wouldn't have so much trouble. Just listen to the tales of woe!

# Payback Time

When people are in love and have stars in their eyes, they don't like to deal with the messy business of contracts. What really gets messy is when the relationship folds and one of the partners realizes too late that she doesn't have a leg to stand on. That's what happened to Amy.

AMY:    When Paul and I met, I was an accountant and he was driving a cab and going to school at night. Since we were planning a life together, we decided that he would go to school full-time and get his degree as a physical therapist. I would pay his tuition and the living expenses, and he'd help out with a part-time job. After he graduated, we'd get married and start a family, and then I would be the one to work part-time. Well, all went as planned, except he split when he graduated. I feel cheated, and I want to sue him for the money I laid out for his tuition. Isn't that fair?

PAUL:    We both went into this relationship believing it was going to work out. I loved Amy. I believe she loved me. We made an arrangement that I would graduate from school early so we could get started on a family. Let me stress here that Amy was the one who really pushed for this arrangement. I was perfectly happy going to school only part-time and paying for it myself. She insisted that it was better for us if I graduated sooner. The relationship didn't work out, and I regret that, but we never had an agreement that this was a loan. Never had a contract, verbal or written, that said if things didn't work out I would owe her a cent.

## Judge Judy Says:

Amy, unfortunately, you should save the cost of filing a lawsuit. In order for you to be successful, you would have to establish that a contract existed between the two of you for Paul to reimburse his tuition and expenses, and there is no contract to that effect. This arrangement was an act of faith in your future, not a contract. Legally, Paul is absolutely right. Consider it money well spent on a good lesson for the future. Next time, make a contract and memorialize your contribution as a loan. That's my legal answer. Don't sue; you'll lose. There are other issues here, too, having to do with common sense and judgment. Amy, since you were chomping at the bit to get started on your life plan together, which included marriage, why didn't you just go ahead and get married? Was something magical going to happen when Paul graduated? You left yourself without any protection whatsoever, because you didn't think things through. Paul, there is no legal claim against you, but that doesn't mean you're off the hook. She put you through school. You'll reap the benefits of her hard work for the rest of your life, and you feel no moral obligation to reimburse her? If that's the case, she's well rid of you.

# Just a Piece of Paper

It's the favorite refrain of gun-shy single people: "A wedding certificate is just a piece of paper!" Does anyone really believe that? Come on! Andrea certainly didn't believe it when Joe, her live-in of five years, tried it on her.

ANDREA:   Joe and I have lived together for five years. We had both been divorced for many years when we met, and now we're in our mid-fifties. Even though he says he loves me and wants to be with me forever, Joe has a "thing" about marriage. He says since we're not planning to have children and we're both mature, it doesn't matter. But it matters to me.

**Just a Piece of Paper**

JOE: We're more committed to each other than most of our married friends. We even wear rings. I just don't see the point. We aren't having children, and we've both been through the marriage thing before. We're perfectly happy just the way we are. Why change it?

## Judge Judy Says:

Do I hear the strains of "It's just a piece of paper?" *You* may be perfectly happy, Joe, but Andrea isn't. If you love her and want to make her happy, you have to respect how important this is to her. Don't tell me that marriage is meaningless. You wouldn't be protesting so much if it were meaningless. I know something about this. After Jerry and I had been dating for about a year, I decided it was time to get married. He, on the other hand, suggested that marriage was merely a piece of paper, the state dictating what the parameters of our lives should be. He, of course, noted that I had already been married, as had he. No one was even suggesting that I was a virgin, so living together would not have created the stir that it might have twenty years earlier. I listened to Jerry's arguments, and I didn't really know how to respond to him. I wasn't looking for a fight. Finally, I suggested that if he was committed to this concept and if he got my father's approval, I'd certainly be willing to go along with it. I knew full well that Jerry was scared to death of my father and would never even pose the question. We were married four months later. Joe, your excuses are weak. The fact that you're both mature and you're not planning to have children has nothing to do with saying "I do." Let me add that with old age creeping up on you, you should be eager to get married. Reliable health care providers are hard to come by.

# It's the Money, Honey

Whenever someone says, "It's not about the money," I guarantee you, that's exactly what it's about—*the money*.

KEVIN:  Martha and I started dating about a year ago. We stopped seeing each other after about six months. While we were dating, Martha asked me to loan her some money. She had fallen behind in her car payments for two months. I trusted her, and I gave her almost $700. A couple of months later, we broke up. She never paid me back, and when I asked her about it, she said she shouldn't have to, because I used the car on the weekends, and it would have cost me more than $700 to rent one. That's beside the point. The money was a loan. She owes me.

**It's the Money, Honey**

MARTHA:  This isn't about the money, and Kevin knows
it. He's bitter because I broke up with him. He
wasn't talking loan when we were together, but
now that we've split up his tune has changed.
Besides, he used my car, too. He should just
leave me alone and get on with his life. I'm
over him; I think he should try to get over me.

## Judge Judy Says:

Martha, stop acting like a princess. You borrowed the
money. Pay it back. Listen up out there in single-world
land: WHEN IT'S A LOAN, GET IT IN WRITING. As a
matter of fact, that's good advice for everyone: family
loans, loans between friends. If you feel embarrassed asking for the written document, just say that Judge Judy insists. Blame me.

# Sharing a Bed

When I was a young woman, I wouldn't have dreamed of
bringing a sleepover of the male persuasion into my parents' home. When I did have a date, my father sat guard
in a straight-backed chair near the front door. If he fell
asleep and I managed to get past him, I'd find my mother
curled up on the couch. No wonder I thought you couldn't

**Sharing a Bed**

get pregnant unless you were married. Today's couples think nothing of demanding a bed together at Mom and Pop's, but their sexually liberated behavior isn't exactly welcome.

JOANNE: Jason and I are both in graduate school and have been living together for two years. When we graduate, we intend to marry. Both Jason's parents and mine know we live together, and though my mother accepts it, my dad refuses to allow Jason and me to sleep together in my room when we visit.

ABE: It's *my*—capital MY—house. My daughter thinks I'm a Neanderthal, and that's her right. But it's *my* right to feel comfortable in my own home, and I am not happy with the prospect that this guy is messing around with my daughter under my roof. If they marry, I suppose I'll have to deal with it, but not until then.

## Judge Judy Says:

Here's the irony: Adult children think it's so "grown-up" to sleep together, but they act like whiny little kids when you suggest they sleep apart for one night. Joanne, I'm with Pop. It is his home, and he sets the ground rules. It's the couch for you, Jason. You can deal with it for a couple of days. If you stay together and get married, there will come a time when having the bed to yourself for a night or two will seem like a luxury.

# Who Pays the Piper?

One of the perks of marriage, as opposed to "just living together," is the divorce. When you are divorcing, there are courts to help you divide your property and settle disputes. There is no "Court of People Just Living Together." It's up to you to be smart. Plan for the eventualities before you set up housekeeping. Keep things simple. Sometimes simple isn't romantic, but often it is very practical. Walking away from a relationship is never easy. Walking away encumbered with debt, bills, leases, and obligations just prolongs the agony.

TOM:    After living together for four years, Julie and I
        split up. We had a lot of outstanding credit
        card bills. We both work, but I earn twice as
        much as she does. We had arranged our
        finances, and I was contributing about double
        what she was to a joint account. We purchased
        many things for our apartment. The lease
        is in my name, and I will be staying in the

apartment. Julie feels that she should be able to walk away free of all debt, and that includes the things that we put on the credit card, such as vacations and expensive dinners.

JULIE:   I contributed to running the household for four years, although Tom paid the majority of the bills. He wants to keep all the furniture. Well, the truth is, I paid for some parts of the furniture with my contribution. So why should I be left with nothing? Tom's going to keep the apartment. He's going to keep all the things that we bought for the apartment. I don't think I should be saddled with any part of the bills.

## Judge Judy Says:

Oh, how we complicate our lives! There will never be a perfect division of assets and liabilities. If Tom is keeping the property and furniture, it's probably equitable for him to assume the outstanding liabilities. Remember, there was a time when you truly cared for each other. Try to make your parting as painless as possible. The expenditure of negative energy over minutiae is like a sickness. Some people thrive on negativity. They usually have deep facial lines and ulcers.

**Who Pays the Piper?**

# On the Dotted Line

A "test run" does not a commitment make.

JOYCE:   Carl and I decided to move in together to see
         if we are compatible. He was living in a small
         studio and I had two roommates. We found an
         adorable place we both liked, and we're ready
         to sign the lease. Suddenly Carl announced
         that he wanted the lease to be in his name
         alone. It's a pretty lousy way to start off a
         commitment, wouldn't you say?

CARL:    Here's my point. Since I am earning more
         money than Joyce, I will be paying the majority
         of the bills. And if this relationship doesn't
         work out, I will probably stay in the apartment,
         because Joyce couldn't afford it alone. It's only
         logical that since we're not married, we
         shouldn't sign a joint lease. That way, if we
         break up—not that I want that to happen—the
         ground rules will be clear.

## Judge Judy Says:

You said it yourself, Joyce: you are moving in to "see if we
are compatible." In other words, you are committed to a
test run. Carl is planning for all eventualities, which is

probably smart. Not romantic, but smart. Think of it this way: If you decide to part company, you can pack and leave unencumbered with a lease you can't afford. You'll be able to start over with no strings or legal hassles. Sounds like a good deal. By the by, Carl sounds pretty decent. He's not afflicted with the split-it-right-down-the-middle mentality. He seems legitimately concerned about you. Maybe he's a keeper.

# Hearts United, Accounts Divided

Sometimes women are in such a rush to pin down a mate that they don't face reality. After a mere six months, Roxanne is sure that Hollis is the one. Since she can't get him to sign a marriage certificate, she figures a credit card is the next best thing. Wrong!

ROXANNE:  Hollis and I started living together last month. We had known each other six months, and I believe we have a shot at a permanent relationship. I think we should do everything as if we were married—joint bank account, joint savings account, and joint credit card. This is the only way to know if we are truly compatible.

HOLLIS:    This is not my first or her first long-term
relationship. I would like to see things
tempered for a while until we are sure that
it's going to work out. This "joint" stuff scares
me to death. Let's try sharing our time. The
"joint" can come later.

## Judge Judy Says:

Hundreds of thousands of cases are filed every year in
small claims courts seeking judicial resolution of the joint
bills accumulated by those who have "tested the waters"
and lived together. Keep it simple and separate until you're
ready to make a commitment—by which I mean marriage.
Even then, Roxanne, you ought to keep a separate account or two. That's the advice I always give to women.
Cherish your independence, even in a relationship.

# Driving Decisions

Remember my laws for live-ins? No major purchases.

GEORGE:    Carol and I lived together for two years. We
purchased a used car for $6,000 and have
been making payments on a loan. There is still
$4,000 left on the loan. We're splitting up, and
I want to keep the car. That's fine with Carol,
but she wants me to reimburse her for what

she paid into the car, which was $1,000. I
think it's unfair. She has had the use of the car
until now, and it has depreciated in value.

CAROL:    I paid for half the car loan, which so far was
$1,000. Also half the repairs and half the
insurance for two years. I can't afford to pay
the loan, so he's welcome to keep the car, but I
must be paid out.

## Judge Judy Says:

Buying joint property without benefit of marriage is
dumb. Sometimes even if you're married it's dumb—but
*always* if you're unmarried. It's too bad you didn't follow
this little gem of advice, Carol. I think the final resolution
should be clear-cut for you: Treat the car as an asset. As-
certain what you could sell the car for, and subtract what
is owed on the loan. The difference is your equity. You
would be entitled to half the equity. If there is no equity,
you'd get nothing. But Carol, darling, make sure your
name is removed from the loan. Some gratuitous advice:
When resolving issues of property, even in a divorce, pay
attention. If an item is financed and you agree to give it
up, make sure you're off the hook for the loan. Do it with
the lending institution, not just with your mate. Otherwise, you may wake up five years later with your credit
damaged because he or she didn't pay off the loan.

# 2

# Tying the Knot

(Ten times measure, one time cut.)

The shape of today's nuclear family often requires fancy footwork when it comes to the wedding. Marvin walked his second wife, Julie, down the aisle at his daughter's wedding. He propped her in the first row, then hustled back to escort his daughter and his first wife down the rose-petal path. At the altar, he kissed his daughter, nodded to Wife One, and took his place in the front row next to Wife Two. Following the ceremony he joined the receiving line, where his three-year-old twin boys from Wife Two insisted that only Daddy could take them to the bathroom. Marvin was sixty-eight. It was an exhausting day.

Welcome to the new nuclear family wedding. Let's face it, families are more complicated than they used to be, and every family has its own can of worms ready to spring open. If you acknowledge this in advance and accept that things might not be precisely the way the fairy tales picture them, you can have a wonderful, meaningful day. But planning is essential to keeping it simple. As my grandmother used to say, "Ten times measure, one time cut." This really is one of my favorite rules. Its origin is the tailor shop, where it was very important to measure a garment correctly before taking the scissors to the fabric. Some things just can't be undone. Too often, people jump into situations without taking a measure of the consequences in advance. They usually get burned. Think—then do!

# Daddy's Big Girl

Multiple marriages with multiple sets of children can create entitlement clashes, as Ken and his daughter Martha found when it came time to discuss her wedding.

KEN:    I am married for the second time and have two young sons. I also have an adult daughter from my first marriage who is getting married.

Martha wants a big wedding. She's a college

graduate and I paid for her education. She has a great job. When she talks about a big wedding, she means something in the neighborhood of thirty to forty grand, and she expects me to pay. Her mother is in no position to help pay for the wedding. I know I always promised Martha I'd give her any kind of wedding she wanted, but my circumstances have changed. I've explained to her that I have two young kids now, and that means additional responsibilities. If she were my only child, I'd move heaven and earth, but she's not, and I expect her to be understanding. Unfortunately, Martha is furious with me.

MARTHA: I understand that Dad has two other children, but I'm only going to have one wedding. We were always so close, and I'm his only daughter, as well as his firstborn. I always assumed that Dad would make me a wedding that would be the day of my dreams. How could he deprive me of that?

## Judge Judy Says:

There are weddings and there are weddings. My first wedding was a big blowout affair, and my father footed the bill. The marriage lasted twelve years. My second wedding was a much smaller affair, but it was one of the loveliest that I've ever attended. So it's not the size, it's not the grandness, it's the feeling and the warmth. Martha, it sounds to me as if you love your dad, and you don't want to add any other stresses to his life. Instead of pressuring him, plan something small that your dad can help with. If you and your intended have jobs and can't live without a big wedding, you can pitch in, too. On a personal note, my father was a super sport. He paid for both of my weddings. After the second, he leaned over and whispered, "The next one's on you, babe." I believed him.

# The Prenup Standoff

People are marrying later today, so the messy issue of prenuptial agreements comes up more often. There is a tremendous amount of emotion centered around this document. Should there be? What's right? Let's listen to Craig and Celeste.

CRAIG:   Celeste knows I love her, and I'm marrying her 'til death, but my lawyer is insisting I have a prenuptial agreement in order to protect my business interests if we should divorce. I don't even want to consider that possibility, but I agree that it would be irresponsible for me to put my business up for grabs. I've told Celeste this is only a formality, but she can't see my side of it at all. Now she's threatening to call off the wedding.

CELESTE: I'm devastated by this whole thing. I think signing a prenuptial agreement is as good as saying we might not make it. What a horrible note to start a marriage. I don't care one whit about Craig's business or his money. He can have it. It's the principle of the thing. If I sign that prenup, our marriage is jinxed.

## Judge Judy Says:

I'd like to see prenuptial agreements become routine. It's an unfortunate fact that 50 percent of all marriages fail, and the courts are clogged with actions for divorces that revolve around two things—property and children. In my experience, the most acrimonious and contentious issues usually involve property, not children. The children are used merely as a tool to get what somebody wants on the property end. Most of these property battles could be resolved by a very simple idea—making prenuptials mandatory. On the marriage license application there can be a section for listing property acquired prior to the marriage, which will not be considered marital property. If you wanted to modify it later, you could. In my mind, this simple change could take away all of the overwrought emotionalism that goes with prenups. Celeste, don't allow your imagination to run away with you. You've manufactured this so-called jinx, but I wonder if you'd feel the same way if prenuptial agreements were required. Probably not.

# Who Gives This Woman?

I'd like to see every parent whose child is getting married repeat this mantra over and over again: *"It's not about me, it's not about me."* Think of the friction it would eliminate. In this scenario, Everett and Shelly are creating unnecessary angst for themselves and their child.

EVERETT:   My daughter is getting married. I have more money than my ex-wife, and I have agreed, I believe graciously, to pay for the wedding. I have been remarried for fifteen years. Both my wife Gail and I work, and our money is joint money. I feel as if my name should be on the invitation since I am paying for the wedding. That's only fair and reasonable. Well, Gail points out that because our joint money is

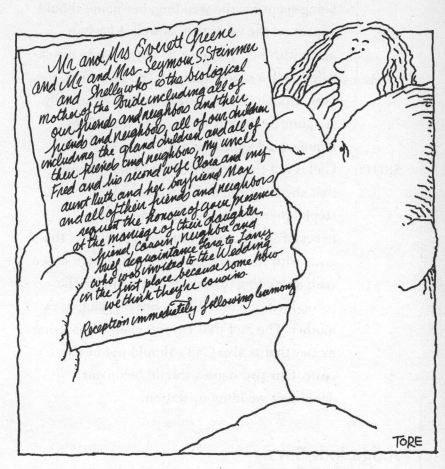

**Who Gives This Woman?**

being spent for the wedding, her name should appear on the invitation as well. I have to agree with her. We have no objection to my ex-wife Shelly's name being on the invitation, too, even though she isn't contributing financially. No surprise, Shelly is outraged that Gail's name would appear at all.

SHELLY:   Gail is not the mother of the bride. I know that she has been a very reasonable stepmother to my daughter. We do not necessarily get along, but that's really not the issue with the wedding invitation. I have never seen a wedding invitation that contains the second wife's name. She is not my daughter's mother. The fact that Everett claims he's using money that is also Gail's should not be the issue. Our two names should be on *our* daughter's wedding invitation.

## Judge Judy Says:

Families get so territorial at wedding time. This is usually the first sticky wicket that the new nuclear family encounters when planning a wedding. Let's cut to the bottom line. Nobody I know saves wedding invitations except the bride and groom. Everybody else tosses them and just saves the directions. So it shouldn't be the first big fight.

How about "The parents of Lara and Larry," or "Lara, Larry, and their parents." Work it out, so your daughter won't have the anxiety of watching you battling over *her* wedding. It's not about money—and it's not about *you*.

# It's My Party

It's not easy being a good mother-in-law. Getting off on the wrong foot before the wedding, *about* the wedding, is a huge error in judgment. Look at Mildred, who wants everybody to be happy, or at least equally unhappy. She's sticking her nose in where it doesn't belong.

MILDRED: My youngest son is getting married. My oldest son is married to a rather difficult woman, who has made it clear that she expects to be the matron of honor at the wedding. When I broached the subject to Patty, my soon-to-be daughter-in-law, she hit the roof. She is an only child and therefore has no sister who would be offended. Why can't she make life easy for everyone?

PATTY: What, are these people nuts? This future sister-in-law is quite a bitch, and my almost-mother-in-law isn't playing with a full deck. It's *my* wedding. I may not have a sister, but I do have a best friend I was planning to ask.

## Judge Judy Says:

Dear June Bride, cool down, but you're right. The choice of your attendant should be yours, but try not to let your righteous indignation start a feud that will continue years into your marriage. Explain to your mother-in-law that you have a special friend who will be your matron of honor. If you want to be a real trooper (something I encourage), tell her you have no problem having the sister-in-law in the wedding party. A word of advice: Try to place your sister-in-law at the end of all photos. She probably won't be around too long and can easily be clipped out without spoiling the photo. In my family, being placed at the end of the family photo is the first clue that you have one foot out the door. Everybody scrambles for the middle seat—so we have great action photos.

# As Good as It Gets

Is it just my imagination, or have young couples today been reading too many fairy tales? Where else would they get such wild expectations about the girl or boy of their dreams? Oh, I know, they call it "high standards." I'd suggest that before they walk down the aisle, the bride and groom should take a healthy dose of reality.

MARK:   Jodie and I are engaged to be married, and
        we're both very happy. However, there are a

few little things that bug me. When I bring
them up, she just gets mad. I know they sound
picky, but they matter to me. For example, she
has very sloppy table manners, she leaves her
makeup all over the bathroom, and she talks to
her mother three times a day. I think Jodie
should care if she's doing things that annoy
me, and try to change them.

JODIE:  Picky is right! If we're making lists, I could
give you a few items from Mark's catalog of
behaviors. Nobody's perfect, and I just can't
believe Mark would make an issue about these
stupid things.

## Judge Judy Says:

Listen up, kids. This time in your romantic relationship is
as good as it will ever get. Right now you have no pres-
sures, none of the hassles of money, children, careers, ill-
ness—all the things that come along to strip the romance
from a marriage. Mark, my advice to you is if there are
things about Jodie that bother you now, just make sure
they're things you can overlook. If the fact that she eats
like an orangutan really irritates you, I guarantee you that
ten years from now you're going to have to wear blinders
at the kitchen table. If it bothers you now that she strews
her makeup all over the bathroom or squeezes the tooth-

paste from the middle of the tube, twenty years from now you're going to want to bury her in toothpaste. If the fact that she talks to her mother three times a day annoys you now, just wait until you have children together and Grandma is popping in and out every day. If you can't accept Jodie's quirks with good humor, I would suggest that you put the skids on the date.

# Processional Tantrums

Whoever said planning the wedding was fun and pleasurable probably had theirs on a polar ice cap surrounded only by seals. Everybody else has aggravation. It's how *much* aggravation that determines the success of the day. That's something you can control, as Frances's mom should see.

FRANCES: I love my grandpa dearly. Two years ago, he married a lovely woman after being a widower for ten years. Though I adored my grandma, I'm thrilled that he is happy and well cared for. Here's the problem: I'm getting married and I'm having a big wedding. I fully intended to have my grandpa and his wife walk down the aisle. When I told my mother, she had a fit.

MOM:     My father and his new wife are happy. She's
         nice, but she's not my mother. People who
         walk down in a wedding procession should be
         the actual parents and grandparents. It's hard
         enough for me not having my mother here to
         see her first grandchild get married. It would
         make it even harder for me to see my father
         and his wife walk down the aisle together.

## Judge Judy Says:

Mom, this question is for you: How many people would
you be making unhappy if you insisted on leaving your father's wife on the sideline? You'd be making your daughter unhappy, and it's her wedding. You'd be making your
father unhappy, because he wouldn't be sharing the moment with his wife. You'd be making your father's wife
unhappy by putting her on the sidelines. That's three.

   Your mother, from wherever she's watching, would
probably want the wedding to be as happy and uncompli-
cated an occasion as possible. Trust me—her feelings
won't be hurt. So the only one you are really considering
is you. Three people would be unhappy, or you could be
unhappy. It seems to me that the math is simple.

# Holy Wars

Jerry and I have five children between us. Four are married. (Yes, at this writing, Gregory is still single, and we are still optimistic.) We are nuts about all of our kids' mates. None of them are of our faith. We kept the ceremonies simple. We performed each wedding ourselves. Unfortunately, not every family has that option.

LILLIAN:    My youngest son just became engaged. We are Jewish. Todd's fiancée is Protestant. Neither family is very religious, but her parents insist on having a minister perform the ceremony.

GENEVIEVE: While it's true that we are not particularly religious, we are Protestants, and in addition to being Protestants we are planning and paying for the wedding. So it seems to me that we have the right to say to the kids that we want a minister to perform the ceremony.

## Judge Judy Says:

My answer is simple: Let the kids decide. Moms, here's the deal. Planning the wedding, arranging the flowers, and deciding whether to have Caesar salad or tossed are not the same as dictating who will perform the ceremony. That is something that should be strictly left up to the children. The color of the linens can be your prerogative. Whether you have a priest, a rabbi, a minister, a monk, or a judge perform the service should be left up to the bride and groom—just as long as it's legal.

# The Last Bash

Personally, I find the good old boys' bachelor party, with drunken bozos cheering as naked women jump out of cakes, to be a distasteful exercise in male bonding. Look what it signifies: The poor groom has been "trapped" into marriage, and this is his last chance for excitement. What hogwash. I am completely sympathetic with anyone who wants to end this particular tradition.

LUCILLE: John and I are getting married in a few weeks, and his friends are intending to have the traditional wild bachelor party for him, complete with hired strippers. It's all sexist and disgusting, and frankly, it makes me sick. John thinks this is all normal stuff, but I'm offended by the whole idea of a roomful of men groping and doing whatever with a couple of "professional" women. As far as I'm concerned, it's degradation and exploitation of women. It's also a lousy way to start a marriage.

JOHN:   Lucille should lighten up. It's all good clean fun. She's trying to turn it into an issue of exploitation of women, but these women advertise their work. They're professionals; they get paid to dance and strip. Besides, I don't expect anything bad to happen at my bachelor party. We're all gentlemen, and the girls have a security guy with them, too. So Lucille is just turning this into an excuse to make the time leading up to our wedding day even more tension-filled than it already is. All of a sudden she's a big feminist. I think she's just a big pain in the ass.

## Judge Judy Says:

I can think of few things less charming than a group of grown men acting like slobbering teenagers before gyrating strippers. Add booze, and you're playing with fire. Why don't you cancel the bachelor party plans and do something different and surprising? Go skiing for the day together, or organize a softball game with your friends. Do something that will bring the two of you closer together, instead of pushing each other away with words.

John, your friends' plans for your bachelor party have created a problem. But you can solve it, and by solving it, you can strengthen your relationship with Lucille. It seems pretty simple to me.

# Adults Only

People who are invited to a wedding should not create trouble for the bride and groom. Whether it's a problem about where they sit, whether they like the food, or whether they bring their children, guests have the responsibility of contributing to a joyful day, not contributing angst. Unfortunately, many people are simply incapable of opening up their needy little hearts for even one day. They've always got to throw a wrench into the works.

LILLY:   Seth and I decided that we didn't want children at our wedding. No one minded at all, except for Seth's cousin Richard. Seth and his cousin are very close. Richard and his wife RSVP'd the invitation and scribbled a note that they would be bringing their two children because they have no one to leave them with. Seth called his cousin and said that we're not having any children at the wedding, and if we allow them to bring their children, a lot of other people will be miffed. They basically said that if their kids couldn't come, they wouldn't come either. Now we don't know what to do.

RICHARD: My cousin Seth should understand our special situation and make allowances. We live 150 miles away from where this wedding is going to be. We're going to travel for the weekend to the wedding, and we don't have anyone we trust to leave our children with. All the other children in the family live much closer, and we think it's not unreasonable for us to ask that an exception be made.

## Judge Judy Says:

Sorry, Richard, but it was really tasteless for you to include your children in your response to the wedding invitation. A much better way would have been to pick up the phone, call Seth, and say, "We have a problem finding a babysitter for our children. Let's see if we can find some way to accommodate that." The bride and groom have elected not to have any children at the wedding, which is their prerogative. Instead of staging a rebellion and making everyone upset, you should quietly make other arrangements. Perhaps your kids could join some of the other children and their babysitter. Or you could stay at a hotel and arrange for a babysitter there. Find a way to attend the wedding and not create problems.

# With This Ring

What happens when the ring, meant to symbolize undying love, doesn't even make it to the altar?

GARY: Janice and I were engaged to be married. We knew each other three years before I proposed and gave her a two-carat ring. Four months before the wedding, I realized it was a mistake and told her so. By then, many of the wedding plans had been made, some with nonrefundable deposits, but I felt that it was better to call off the wedding than to make a mistake I'd regret the rest of my life. I think Janice should return the ring, which is the proper thing to do. She says I can have the ring back if I give her parents the money they laid out for the wedding.

JANICE: I was not only heartbroken but humiliated when Gary called off the wedding, and my parents are out thousands of dollars. If he wants the ring back he can have it, but let's see some responsibility here.

## Judge Judy Says:

Janice, the ring was given as a gift in expectation that a marriage would take place. It should rightfully be returned to Gary, even if he called off the wedding. (Think of the consequences if he went through with the wedding just because the flowers had been ordered!) I certainly believe he should reimburse your folks for some of their expenses. It would be the right thing to do. If he needs the money, he can always sell the ring. However, let me give you a piece of advice: Let it go. As long as you hold the ring hostage, your heart and mind will be hostage, too. You need to move on.

# 3

# Married Bliss

**(If life were fair, men would have stretch marks.)**

Congratulations, you survived the ceremony. Now comes the fun part—living. It can be fun, too, if you lighten up your expectations. It can also be work, along with periods of boredom. Some newlyweds just aren't ready to crash down to earth. I once saw a television report about women who were literally in mourning because their wedding day was over. They would spend hours replaying the video, and even wear their wedding dresses around the house. Obviously, for them, the thrill of their lives was walking down the aisle. *Getting* married was great; *being* married was another matter.

Marriage is for adults. Once the bloom has worn off the rose, you'll need more than romance to hold you together and keep you happy. A special caution for women: As you settle into a routine, you may foolishly expect a fifty-fifty division of responsibility around the house. Battle lines are drawn unless there is a quick adjustment in expectations. Take it from one who's been there and made some serious missteps: Neither expect nor demand equality. Figure out what ratio you can live with. Look at your mate as you would a piece of meat: There's a center filet—the best part. There's a somewhat tougher section surrounding the center, and there's the gristle. My suggestion is to concentrate on the filet, but make pretty damn sure there *is* one.

# Learned Helplessness

In my last book, *Beauty Fades, Dumb Is Forever*, I discussed the concept of "learned helplessness." This is an affliction that strikes men once they have been mated with women. Suddenly, perfectly intelligent and capable males, who have been scrambling eggs and washing socks on their own for years, can't negotiate boiling water. The part of the brain that controls domestic chores has been wiped clean.

SARAH:    Christopher and I have been married for almost two years now. We both have careers

**Learned Helplessness**

and are very busy. We get up at the same time
each morning and get off work at the same
time each evening. What's happened is that
I've become the "doer," and Christopher has
become completely unable or unwilling to
handle anything for himself. I don't
understand it, because before we were married
Christopher seemed able to handle all of his
own affairs—apartment cleaning, vacuuming,
laundry, dry cleaning, shopping, cooking,
making appointments with the doctor—all by
himself. Now he's become a helpless imbecile.
I'm even in charge of buying gifts for his
family and friends for their birthdays.
Christopher can't make a doctor's appointment
for himself; he can't shop for food, wash or
dry-clean his own clothes, make the bed. It's
as though our getting married gave him
permission to just kick back and have a
personal slave. This started within the first
year of our marriage, and, of course, I put my
foot down. I told Christopher, "I can't do
everything for you that you used to do for
yourself. It's bad for me, and it's bad for you. I
resent it, and it builds up a lot of frustration
and rage in me." He agreed, and promised that
he would make an effort to take care of his

share of chores, personal appointments, and other responsibilities. He did it for five or six months, and nothing got done. His parents' anniversary went unnoticed, and guess what? They blamed me. He forgot his nephew's birthday, he ran out of socks, and our electricity got shut off because he didn't get around to paying the bill. Now what? It's so unfair for me to be saddled with all of the chores, but it's either that or nothing gets done.

CHRISTOPHER: I'm perfectly prepared to assume my prior responsibilities. That's not the issue. But Sarah has to understand that we do things differently. I'm certainly not as efficient or as organized as she is; I wish that I were. If there are things I'm doing that she feels she can handle more efficiently, then by all means, she should take on those things herself. You know, if you don't like the way I'm doing something, do it yourself.

## Judge Judy Says:

Christopher, climb down off of the Jungle Gym in the back yard, and come into the house of reality, where the grownups live. Let me ask you something.

What would you say to an employee who told you, "It doesn't matter what kind of a job I do, as long as I do it"? I'm guessing that person wouldn't last five minutes. Yet that's what you're telling Sarah. To me, it sounds like a ploy to get her to take over all the chores. Sarah, tread carefully here. In the early stages of a marriage, it's easy to become the one who takes care of all of a couple's chores. I think that most women do take most of the responsibilities onto themselves for couples-related activities, like socializing with family and friends, making medical and dental appointments, grocery shopping, laundry, housekeeping, bill paying, and the buying of gifts and sending of cards for birthdays and anniversaries. A lot of women also begin to resent it after a while, especially when they're holding down full-time jobs. Whatever you do now, when there are just the two of you, is a precursor of what is to come when the children arrive. If Christopher has a case of "learned helplessness" now, imagine how inept he'll become when there are diapers to change!

It's a trap for women, and most of us fall into it, simply because our mates aren't as adept or as reliable as we are. All they have to do is emphasize their inability to handle anything once or twice, and strategically, the war of responsibility is over. They become the reclining, relaxed victors, while we become the *schleppers*—doing everything we can to make everyone happy and comfortable so some peace prevails. We're the losers in the responsibility sweepstakes, and our "can't rely on me" husbands are the winners. These kinds of conflicts are a part of every marriage. It comes under the category of trying to make the person you married behave the way you want them to behave, rather than the way that they do. So if you're a man and you can get your wife to handle all the things you want to avoid, well, life can be pretty much a free ride. The time to nip it in the bud is now. There's still time.

# The Three Musketeers

You can't go into a marriage on automatic pilot, assuming everything will be fine. Love doesn't conquer all; you need ground rules, too.

CARYN:   My new husband has two very close buddies, both unmarried guys his age. He's twenty-seven years old, and I'm twenty-three. These guys used to be like the Three Musketeers, and they still basically behave that way. Joseph's friends think nothing of just dropping in, which they both do all of the time. They don't phone; they just show up. They're constantly hanging around, and they have no

**The Three Musketeers**

qualms about interfering in our life, staying for
meals, acting like it's old times. I feel like I'm
now married to three guys, two of whom I find
really obnoxious, and the worst part of this
whole thing is, Joseph sees nothing wrong with
it. How can I convince him that things have
changed—without having all three of them
thinking I'm a bitch?

JOSEPH: Just because I'm married, I shouldn't have to
give up my friends. Besides, how is this any
different from Caryn yakking on the phone for
two hours with her girlfriends? She thinks
nothing of taking phone calls in the middle of
dinner or when we're alone together, but she
accuses me of spending too much time with
my buddies. She liked them fine before we
were married.

## Judge Judy Says:

You're both a little bit right and a little bit wrong. Joseph,
there's no reason why you have to give up your friends,
but now that you're married, be more considerate of your
wife's need for privacy. I know I resent unannounced vis-
itors in my home—even relatives. The other two Musketeers have to be told to call in advance, and visit at your
and Caryn's convenience. At the same time, Caryn, chat-

ting on the phone for hours on end can be intrusive to Joseph, too. It sounds to me as if the two of you should decide on some simple ground rules for relating to friends.

# Mother-in-Law Blues

To say that families complicate marriage is an understatement. In-laws, siblings, cousins, holidays, all wreak havoc on the notion of keeping it simple. Before I married my first husband, my mother wisely said, "Don't just look at the boy. You're marrying the whole family." It was good advice. When it comes to mothers-in-law, I think they've gotten a bad rap. How can all terrific, caring mothers suddenly transform into selfish, conniving troublemakers overnight? Now that I hold that title myself, I like to think that I'm a wonderful mother-in-law. However, it's the nature of families that loyalties are tested when new members come along.

IRENE:    Sal's mother is a complete downer. She's
          negative, critical, and whenever she's around,
          she makes me miserable. She makes it clear
          that she believes I'm the luckiest lady alive to
          have snared her sainted son. She gives me
          unsolicited advice about everything from

decorating to childrearing. I think it's Sal's place to tell her to stop harassing me and mind her own business.

SAL: Oh, come on, she's an old lady with an attitude. Give her a break. I'm an only child, and I was born late in my parents' life. They always doted on me. I'm the only one in my family who ever graduated from college, so they think I'm a really big deal. My wife, as it happens, has a master's degree, but that doesn't matter to my mother. I admit that she can be hard to take at times, but frankly, it's too late for Mom to change, so what's the point of confronting her about it? It would only make matters worse.

## Judge Judy Says:

Sal, I suspect that what really bothers Irene is not so much your mother's attitude as the feeling that you're not her ally in this. If Irene's perception is that it's you and your mother on one side and she's on the other, she's going to be rightfully resentful. On the other hand, if you let Irene know that you appreciate the fact that your mother is in the wrong, your mother's behavior will probably bother her less. In my experience, it's only when a husband or wife tries to be overly protective of their parents at the spouse's expense that resentment flourishes. So to both of you, I would say, lighten up a bit. If the two of you together can poke fun at, as you call her, the old lady with an attitude, I think it will make it easier to have her around. That doesn't mean she has to be a constant visitor. Try to keep the visits of short duration and in a neutral place. Sal, I wish I had a direct line to your mother, but from what you say, that line has been disconnected.

# Tomorrow and Tomorrow

Often people discover qualities about their partner only after the wedding. Sometimes the surprises are unpleasant.

CHAD:   Before we were married, Julie and I took care of our own bills. Now we have a joint account and she wants to handle the finances. The problem is, she doesn't pay the bills as they come in. Piles of mail and unopened bills can sit around for a week. It drives me crazy. She says she'll get to it, and usually does, but occasionally we get a second notice or a finance charge. Our lives are busy, but I'm more than willing to handle the finances myself and take care of the bills. But she's adamant about doing it herself.

JULIE:    My husband has a touch of Obsessive-
Compulsive Disorder. Everything gets done
eventually, when I have the time. Visa won't go
out of business, nor will our credit rating be
destroyed forever, if I'm a week late paying the
bill. I wish Chad wouldn't get so worked up
over nothing.

## Judge Judy Says:

Chad and I must suffer from the same affliction. It's the
"don't put off 'til tomorrow what you can do today" syndrome. I'm a big believer in organizing those things that
can be organized. Life has a way of throwing an occasional curve ball. I find that the best way of coping with
the unanticipated is to keep what can be organized, organized. So Julie, I side with Chad. If you want to be responsible for paying the bills, pay them when they arrive.

# Money Matters

Just because you're in love doesn't mean you'll be in
agreement. I've never known a couple that didn't have
some kind of conflict about money. Most of these conflicts could be avoided if people would simply discuss
money matters before the wedding. It may not be roman-

tic, but do you really want to wake up and find that your financial priorities are on opposite ends of the spectrum?

ANNETTE: Kurt was Mr. "The-Sky's-the-Limit" when we were dating. Now that we're married, he's turned into Mr. Scrooge. Every time I spend a penny, he's all over me like a cheap suit. I can't even buy a pair of shoes without having to put up with his griping. Excuse me, but I am an adult woman with a very good job. I'm hardly a spendthrift, but I think I have a right to spend some of my income as I please.

KURT:    We're trying to save up to buy a house, and she drops $200 on a pair of shoes. So yes, I get annoyed. We're in this together, but Annette doesn't seem to be very serious about saving.

## Judge Judy Says:

It's too late for me to say that you should have hammered out the money issues before the wedding. Kurt, you were too busy trying to dazzle Annette. Annette, you were too busy having a ball. Now it's time to come down to earth and work on the family budget. If you've never done a budget before, there are plenty of books to help you. Having said that, let me add a note. Kurt, you may not like

this, but I believe that every woman should have an independent bank account that is hers alone. If she wants to
spend $200 on a pair of shoes, so be it. If she wants to
save for a rainy day, that's okay, too. Men shouldn't feel
threatened when their wives are financially independent.
*My* husband loves it!

# Holiday Headaches

Holidays present one of those complicated yours-mine-
ours setups that cause no end of grief in families.

JILL:      Don and I have been married for three
           months, but we've been together almost two
           years. Don is an only child. I have two sisters
           who are married. We live at least 500 miles
           from the nearest parent. The Christmas
           holidays are approaching, and we're having our
           first major fight of the marriage. Don says that
           it's only reasonable to spend the holidays with
           his parents since he's their one and only. If we
           use that logic, I'll never spend Christmas with
           my family again. We spent Christmas with
           Don's parents last year. It's my turn.

DON:       I just don't see any way to resolve this
           problem. Jill has a large family, and I enjoy

being with them. But how can I leave my parents all alone over the holidays? I'd feel terrible.

## Judge Judy Says:

When two people are trying to do the right thing, as you both are, there's always a way. Let's look at this rationally. Jill can't be expected to forgo holidays with her parents forever. That's unreasonable. At the same time, Don is trying to be a devoted son. Let's think creatively. Don, maybe you could invite your parents to join you and Jill's family for the holidays, and both families could be together. Or maybe the families could select a third, neutral location, like a resort. Many couples solve the problem by alternating Thanksgiving and Christmas, then switching the following year. Instead of trying to do things the way they have always been done, start a new tradition. Compromise is imperative in keeping a marriage together, and holidays always come around once a year. They should be a time of joy and togetherness, not perpetual divisiveness.

# Hawaiian Baggage

JOANNE:  It's going to be our tenth anniversary soon, and after years of cajoling and plotting, I got my

**Hawaiian Baggage**

husband, Jimmy, to agree to a trip to Hawaii to celebrate. Without the kids, mind you. It's our first vacation alone since the kids were born. Jimmy came home yesterday and told me, out of the blue, that he invited his brother and his wife to join us. I just looked at him like he grew an extra head, and then I was all over him like a rash. We had a huge fight. Now we're not talking to each other. How can he be so insensitive? We *need* this time alone.

JIMMY:   Look, it's not like I *invited* them. My brother and his wife have been going through a very rough period, and my brother suggested that it might really help them to get away. He asked if they could tag along. What was I going to do, say no? Frankly, I don't see why it's such a big deal. It's not as if we'll be sharing a room.

## Judge Judy Says:

Jimmy, you're clueless. While you're so busy trying to save your brother's marriage, your wife is getting ready to pack her bags. Your brother and his wife can mend their marriage at another locale. It doesn't have to be Hawaii. Besides, since when do husbands make social plans? It's not unreasonable for Joanne to want to celebrate a special anniversary alone, and that's what you should do.

# It's My Turn

When my children were young, I put my career on the back burner in order to stay home and nurture them full-time. When they started school, I dusted off my gray suit, got a wonderful job, and the fight was on. I thoroughly expected my husband to give me 100 percent of his support. I was disappointed when he balked, and that disappointment led to resentment. In today's two-parent working households, there is never an equal division of responsibilities as far as house and children and shopping and social managing. Most men will agree that they're getting away with murder. However, they will only acknowledge that privately to themselves while singing in the shower, as the breakfast is being prepared downstairs by their working spouse.

GREG:   I have a very demanding job. I earn good money and I've always supported our family well. Sandy wants to go back to work now that the kids are in school, and that's okay with me. But suddenly she expects me to help out in the mornings and take time off work to pick up the slack. Since I'm the primary breadwinner, I don't think I should be put in this position.

SANDY:   I'm serious about my work, and I already gave up eight years to stay home with the kids. We agreed that when the kids were in school, I'd resume my career. Greg is being selfish and thoughtless, which is nothing new. There have been times during the last few years when I have been so frustrated by the sheer weight of the routine of my life, I could just scream. Greg walks in each evening at around 7:30 P.M., tired and rumpled, but still looking so neat in his suit and tie, his briefcase all clean and ordered. Everything's quieted down by then. He has no idea what goes on in a house full of little kids each day. Now I need him to pitch in—not a lot, but some. One would think I'd asked him to bear children the way he's screaming.

## Judge Judy Says:

Changing established patterns is hard, especially when one spouse is perfectly comfortable with the old format. Greg, when you made your agreement with Sandy that she would stay home when the kids were young and resume her career when they started school, what did you think that meant? Did your cooperation hinge on her willingness to do everything—manage a job plus all the household duties? My guess is that you didn't think about it. You assumed your life would be the same, no matter what. It's time for you to reevaluate the concept of a partnership. Sandy is not asking you to scrub the floor on your hands and knees, just to help her get breakfast ready once in a while. So roll up your sleeves and do the right thing.

# Retiring Ways

Couples who have been married for thirty or forty years think they know each other so well—until retirement.

HARRIET: Harold and I have been married for thirty-seven years. He's always run his own business, and I always stayed home and ran the house. It's been an excellent arrangement. He's always been extremely busy with his work, and over the years, I developed a tremendous number of my own interests. Of course, I always took care of all of the social functions surrounding the business, of which there were many. I became an excellent organizer, and extended my expertise into other areas. I've managed to become involved in a lot of volunteer work, and developed friendships with women in similar positions to mine. I have a very active "work" life of my own, and now that the children are grown and out of the house, I've devoted myself to my very favorite causes. Which brings me to my problem. A few months ago, Harold retired. After over forty years with his company, he decided at last to slow down. The problem is, his idea of retirement is for us to spend all of our time together. I love Harold, but I don't love his version of retirement. I feel as though I've got a new child in my life—"Where are you going? What are we going to do today? Can I go with you?" It's driving me nuts. I'm like a social director, trying to plan out each of his days, fill them up with interesting things to do and interesting places to go. My driven business-leader husband has reverted into this boring, doesn't-know-what-to-do-with-himself old man, and he expects me to keep him company!

HAROLD:  I'm feeling very depressed by my wife's response to my retirement. We always talked about retirement. It was what we'd worked for—the time we could be together and enjoy ourselves. But Harriet isn't happy at all. I can see that she's always sighing and shaking her head, as if having me around is really a tremendous burden on her. I say, "Hey, let's go out, play a few holes of golf, then have lunch at the club!" Her response is always the same: "Oh, I can't. I have a committee meeting of the museum board today"—or whatever, and off she goes. On Tuesdays it's the theater; on Thursdays she attends the ballet; Wednesdays she plays tennis with some of her girlfriends; Fridays she has a painting class, and there's a cooking class some other day. In other words, her life is already perfectly full without me. I'm one of those guys who devoted all of my interest to my business for more than forty years, and I was looking forward to our "golden years" together. Is that so unreasonable?

## Judge Judy Says:

Let's put things in perspective. You're an incredibly lucky couple. You both still seem to have your health, your minds, and the means to do as you wish. Everything else can be worked out, with a little massaging and some good old-fashioned compromise. Harriet, your man is alive, kicking, and raring to go, and you're *kvetching* about him. Meet him halfway. In other words, make room for Daddy, darling. In all fairness to him, he, thank God, loves you and wants to spend time with you, so make an effort. If that means cutting back on a few of your social obligations, resigning from a couple of committees, so be it. Carve out some time for Harold; plan a vacation or two together. Enroll in a film course together, or any kind of class that the two of you might enjoy. One day each week go watch a film, then discuss it. Or better yet, Harriet, maybe you can form your own group. Use your organizational skills to create a group for women with husbands who've retired. There are plenty of women like you out there, wives with husbands in need of attention and some new friends. Create a name for it: Old Boys Without Friends. The Retired Men's Club. Something that will help take some of the pressure off you. I'll tell you what else works: computers. Buy your husband a computer, then hire an expert to teach him how to use it. Enroll him in the local gym, and hire a trainer to make sure he goes there and works out a few times every week. Good for him, correct? It will help to keep him alive longer, as well as feeling better and looking better. Good for you, too, as a way of getting him out from underfoot. Men are notoriously bad at organizing this kind of thing.

That's just one of the reasons that God created women. So make dates for him until he starts getting used to this new routine you're both trying to adjust to. It's all about finding a new balance in your relationship. Make the effort to enjoy these good years, and enjoy them together, as partners. That's a court order.

# 4

# Kids Happen

(Having a baby is easy; being a parent is hard.)

Every child has the right to enter the world wanted by two parents who are committed to loving, nurturing, and supporting him or her. All too often, children are conceived with some ulterior purpose, their welfare merely an afterthought. People get all caught up with the idea of passing on their brilliant one-of-a-kind genes, without considering the consequences—that this is a real live human being who doesn't arrive in the world an instant genius. There's another dynamic, too—and here I'm talking to women. If you're having a baby to keep a marriage together, to snag a man, to build your self-esteem, or because you feel you need a small companion, you're committing an act of stupidity and irresponsibility. I've never met the baby who saved a marriage that was failing. The decision to have children must be thoughtfully made by two people. It has to be about the child more than it is about you. I'm always amazed by couples who have been together for years (often "on and off") who decide to have children together. When I ask why they didn't get married before announcing the blessed event, they reply, "We're not ready to make that kind of permanent commitment." And they're serious!

# Seminal Fraud

How many times have I heard people say, "I meant well"? Usually I take that to mean, "I meant well for my own needs." As far as I'm concerned, fraud is fraud, and that's what Jane perpetrated on the unsuspecting Peter.

PETER:    My wife and I have been married for four years, and we were always unable to have a child. My world opened up for me when I came home one day six months ago and Jane told me she was pregnant. I thought it was a miracle. But things have changed over the last few months. We just weren't getting along. We decided we were basically unsuited, and we started divorce proceedings. Then Jane broke

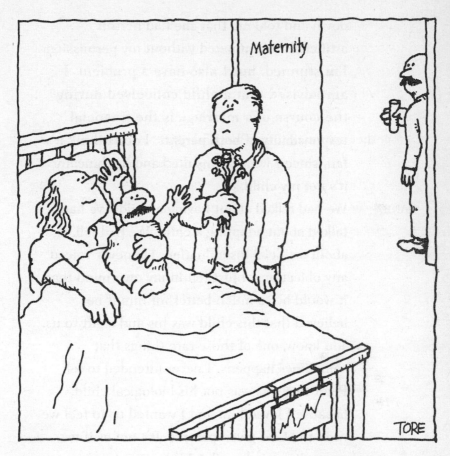

**Seminal Fraud**

down and told me that she had herself
artificially inseminated without my permission.
I'm stunned, but I also have a problem. I
am advised that a child conceived during
the course of a marriage is the financial
responsibility of both parents. I don't think it's
fair, since I wasn't consulted and, technically,
it's not my child.

JANE:   We had talked about having a child. We had
talked about adopting a child. We had talked
about artificial insemination. He never voiced
any objections. I just felt in my own mind that
it would be so much better for him if he
believed that this child was his and a gift to us.
You know, one of those rare things that
sometimes happens. I never intended to tell
Peter that this was not his biological child,
because I loved him and I wanted us to feel we
were the God-given parents. It's not as if we
never discussed artificial insemination. He
wasn't necessarily opposed to it. I just never
told him I did it.

## Judge Judy Says:

Jane, without hitting you over the head about your poor
judgment in perpetrating this disgraceful fraud on your

spouse, the financial support of this child would be yours alone if I were the judge. Although there is a presumption that a child born during the marriage is the child of both parties, this presumption can be overcome in this case by DNA testing. Foolproof. Let me put it another way. Since there was no consent, to me it would be no different than if you'd had an extramarital affair in order to become pregnant, not telling Peter about it, and pretending the child conceived was his.

# His, Mine, and Ours

Carmen and Bill entered their marriage with an agreement: No more kids. Since they already had four between them, this wasn't unreasonable. Now Carmen is playing the woman's prerogative card. She's changed her mind, and Bill isn't buying it.

BILL:   When Carmen and I married she had two children, ages five and six, and I had two children, ages four and seven. My former wife is primary custodian of my two children, but I support them, and they're with us two weekends a month and during the summer. Before we got married, Carmen and I agreed that four children was enough. Well, two years go by, and Carmen starts talking about wanting a baby that's *ours*. Our finances are strapped enough as they are. We both work just to keep up with expenses. The way I see it, children are children. I love her kids and she loves mine. Why do we have to go through a period now where we would be having a new baby? Carmen would have to give up her job, at least for part of the time, or cut back, or we'd have the additional child care expense. But it's not just the money. I think our family is fine just as it is.

CARMEN: Before we were married, I didn't know I would feel this way. Maybe it's just an emotional thing with me, but it's very real. Bill and I love each other so much, and I just feel as if it would make my life complete if we had one child biologically together.

## Judge Judy Says:

Carmen, I understand where you're coming from emotionally. You love this man, and you feel it would be the ultimate fulfillment of your marriage if you created a child with him. Before your dig in your heels on this point, think it through. What effect would a new baby have on your children, your financial stability, your lifestyle as a family? According to Bill, you are already feeling pretty stretched financially. Don't underestimate the strain that financial pressure places on a marriage—especially a new one. Think of what your life would be like if you had a new baby. If you wanted to stay home for a while with that baby, you would have only one income. If Bill had to get a second job, it would take him away from the family and would exhaust him in the bargain. When my husband, Jerry, and I married, I had two children, Jerry had three, and they were all quite young. I was working full-time and Jerry was working full-time, plus moonlighting as a judge at the Parking Violations Bureau three nights a week just to make ends meet. And there was a period when I really wanted us to have a child together. I was thirty-four and Jerry was forty-two. We were certainly young enough. Although I think I wanted a baby more than he did, Jerry went along. It never came about, and now that I look back with 20–20 hindsight, I think we had a perfect family just as it was. I also realize that if I'd had another child, that child would have been only nine or ten when I turned forty-five, which was the year I became a grandmother for the first time. When I had my first grandchild, did I love to play with that baby, and was I happy when that baby went home. I slept through the night. I didn't have measles and chicken pox and croup and all the other things that go along with being a full-time parent.

# Baby Roulette

Here is another variation on the same theme.

ROGER:    I'm forty-six. When I was younger, I had a testicular problem, which I was told would probably render me unable to have biological children. I've been in a long-term relationship with Ann for the last nine years. She is in her mid-forties, has a very successful career, and she never planned to have children. Well, lo and behold, last month Ann wasn't feeling well, so she went to the doctor, and the doctor told her that she was pregnant. One of those little guys that I didn't think could make it apparently did. I have to say, I was pretty excited. Unfortunately, Ann wasn't. She reminded me that she never wanted children, and didn't plan on getting pregnant. The bottom line is that she doesn't want to tie herself down to a child in her mid-forties. I can't believe she could even think of not having this baby. It's a wonderful gift.

ANN:    Let me tell you about Mr. Father of the Year. Roger's perception of commitment is Wednesday and Saturday dinner, one or two weeklong vacations a year, and remembering my birthday. He has made it clear over the last nine years that he likes his routine and his privacy. Notice that nowhere does he mention marriage. He's only interested that his lonely little sperm scored a touchdown. The decision about this baby is mine.

## Judge Judy Says:

Sorry, Roger, Ann is right. The decision's hers—even if you were a candidate for Father of the Year. You clearly weren't committed to her before. From the tone of your letter, while she accepted it, she had hoped for more. A child is a gift that requires commitment. A word to Ann: Think long and hard before you make this decision. A child can change your life in magical ways you wouldn't believe.

# Boys Will Be Boys

Richard and Amanda are caught in a classic parenting struggle. They disagree about discipline. Is Amanda too harsh, or is Richard blind?

RICHARD: Our seven-year-old son's second-grade teacher has called several times to complain about his behavior in class, and we've been brought in for conferences with the school psychologist and the teacher. What a waste of time. There's nothing wrong with Jason. He's a high-spirited boy. Like all boys, he can be a little rambunctious, but that's only normal. My opinion is that this young teacher doesn't know how to handle boys. They aren't like little girls—all sweet and well-behaved. I'm glad Jason's got some spunk.

AMANDA: My husband always makes excuses for our son with his boys-will-be-boys attitude. He basically gives Jason permission to behave badly, practically goads him into it when he's around him at home, and I think it's impacted negatively on his behavior at school. We should be the ones to take care of this, starting with some increased discipline and responsibilities around the house. We can't just blame this young teacher.

## Judge Judy Says:

I heard the expression, "He'll grow up soon enough," for years as a judge in the Family Court. I saw the "accidental" firecracker that takes out an innocent eye, and the "playful" joyride in a stolen car. Where do we think troubled kids come from? They don't spring fully formed from the briar patch. Scratch a disrespectful kid and you're likely to find an overly permissive parent. It's never too soon to begin to mold your child into a responsible citizen. Playing catchup can be costly, financially and emotionally. As my grandmother used to say, "Better he should cry now than you should cry later." Richard, you're a fool. This young teacher has better things to do than to pick on your child. She's trying to help you. Your wife understands that, and it's your responsibility to support her and the teacher. Be a parent, not a buddy.

# Running Amok

Debbie and Lucille are sisters. They've been at each other's throats for many years, and their current problem is just the latest in a long list of skirmishes.

**DEBBIE:**   My sister has four-year-old twin boys, and they don't know how to behave—in their home or mine. I don't really blame *them* because they're just little kids. Lucille sets no boundaries for them whatsoever. She doesn't ever tell them no, or discipline them. When they visit my house, she sits there chatting away, ignoring them while they run wild. I usually end up being the one to tell them to settle down, and then Lucille goes ballistic. She'll do one of those "How dare you speak to my children in that tone of voice" numbers. We'll end up arguing, and the boys take it all in. Don't I have a right to say something in my own house?

LUCILLE: It's easy for Debbie to be so high and mighty. She doesn't have kids, and she probably never will. Obviously, she doesn't like kids. She never misses an opportunity to lecture them. By the way, ever since we were little, Debbie has always acted like she was better than me, and this is just one more example.

## Judge Judy Says:

First of all, this argument is not really about the kids, is it? You two sound like you'd manage to find something to fight about no matter what. That being said, it isn't unreasonable to want one's home left standing after children come to visit—and it's the parents' obligation to set the boundaries. Debbie, you have a right to be comfortable in your own home, so why don't you start visiting Lucille in her home, or meet in a neutral place like a park? Maybe when the kids get older and can behave more respectfully, you can invite them over. But for now, why give yourselves this golden opportunity to be annoyed? Meanwhile, Lucille, a piece of advice for you: The word "no" is not bad. It may surprise you to learn that many parenting authorities say that children actually appreciate being reined in when they get out of hand. They don't know how to set limits for themselves; they're counting on you to do it.

# Kids' Rights

Every generation of parents has its share of worries, but it's fair to say that the present generation has a few fears that never would have been imagined thirty years ago. Kids have access to dangerous and adult materials, through the Internet and other media. They have access to drugs, and some of them, tragically, have access to guns. Parents of teens are rightfully unnerved, and they feel a legitimate need to be on top of what is going on in their children's lives. Naturally, this extra attention doesn't sit too well with the teens.

DAMIEN:    I am fourteen, and I think my room should be
           my room, private, only for me. I'm a good
           student, and I've never been in any trouble.
           Ever since those school shootings and all the
           talk about drugs, my parents have been

watching me like a hawk. I've never done any drugs or anything, but they believe they can come into my room without permission whenever they want. When we had a fight about it, my stepdad finally said, "This is our house, not yours, and we'll look at anything in your room we want to look at anytime." I was so mad. The next day, after school, I put a deadbolt lock on my bedroom door. It cost me almost $60, but I thought it was worth it. When my parents got home later that day and saw what I'd done, they went nuts. They had a locksmith take it off. Why can't they trust me?

DEBRA:   Raising a teenager today, with the kinds of things that are taking place, is an unsettling experience, to put it mildly. As a parent, it's not only my right, but it's also my duty to make sure he's not in any trouble or in any danger. We've seen so many examples of parents not paying attention, and before you know it, their kids are in trouble. I know Damien resents the intrusion, but that's just the way it's going to be.

## Judge Judy Says:

Debra, keep that locksmith's number handy, just in case Damien gets any other bright ideas. Put the locksmith on a retainer if you have to. It's your duty to know what's going on with your son, and he may not be happy now, but maybe he'll thank you later. It seems as if Damien is a good kid, and you've done something right so far. As long as he knows that his room is not off-limits to you, it will help him resist temptations. When I was still working in Family Court, a bailiff, a woman I worked with, approached me one day. We always asked after one another's children. On this particular day, I vividly remember what she said, referring to her two boys. She was a tough, no-nonsense, hardworking single mother, and she said, "Let me tell you something, Judge. In my house, I *own* the air they breathe. I'm going to do everything I can to make sure my kids don't end up hanging with the wrong crowd, or ever bring anything into my house that's trouble. The only way I'm ever going to find any of this out is to have access to every square inch of my place. I pay the rent. I can look anywhere anytime I want. If they want privacy, they can have privacy. Go get a job, rent their own apartment, then they'll have privacy. As long as they breathe the air that I pay for, eat the food I buy, read by my light and watch my television using my electricity, then I set the rules." It was a great speech, and I replied enthusiastically, "You go for it!" So that's what I say to you, Debra: Go for it. You own the air. Damien, your right to privacy will begin when you move out of their home and into a space of your own.

# The Full Nest Syndrome

Remember when everyone was talking about the "empty nest syndrome"? We don't hear too much about that anymore because the kids are not leaving—and when they do leave, they come back.

CHRISTINE: All three of our grown boys are still living at home. Freddie is twenty-two, and the twins, Billy and Bob, are both twenty-one. I'm still their maid, chief cook, and laundress. I was looking forward to a little peace and privacy. The boys are also always fighting over who gets to use our second car, which usually results in our being stranded without a car. Freddie graduated from college last year, but he hasn't decided what to do with his $100,000 degree. He spends a lot of time over at his girlfriend's house or tying up our phone talking to her. Bill and Bob attend community college, although for some reason I can't fathom, Bob is taking the semester off. It's not to work, I can tell you that. I want the boys out of the house if they're not going to go to work or go to school. My husband's the problem. Even though both of us have good jobs and work hard, he doesn't criticize our sons at all for just hanging around. He seems to get a kick out of it, like they're all buddies or something. He says they're young, let them enjoy themselves.

RALPH: Christine is overdramatizing. Our sons are good boys. They'll be fine. What are we supposed to do, throw them out into the streets? It's not like it was when we were kids. Once you got out of high school, you were basically on your own. Not today. Kids stay home longer than they used to. I don't think it's necessarily a bad thing. They're young. Give them time.

## Judge Judy Says:

When all of our children finished their schooling, Jerry and I moved into a small apartment for a year. It made the not-so-subtle statement to the kids: You're not coming to live with us. Visit, yes. Reside, no. Ralph, it's time for you and your wife to devote time to each other, and to nudge your boys into responsible adulthood.

# Religious Ties

The wisdom of Solomon might come in handy when it comes to settling matters of religion in mixed families. In this case, Grace thought the matter of how to raise the children *was* settled—until children became a reality.

RAY:    Grace and I have been married for three years and we're expecting our first child—a boy. I'm Jewish, Grace is Catholic. Neither of us is particularly religious, so when we discussed religion prior to the wedding, I agreed that our children would be raised in the Catholic faith. Now that a baby is on the way, my parents are devastated, and I'm caught in the middle. I have suggested that we give our child a taste of both religions and let him decide later. My folks are satisfied with this, my wife is not.

GRACE:  It's not as if we didn't discuss religious issues before we were married. While it's true that I am not religious, my parents are, and that is the reason I wanted to settle the issue of children and religion before the wedding. Ray's parents, who haven't set foot in a synagogue in years, as far as I know, are now interfering with an issue that has already been settled, and I resent it.

## Judge Judy Says:

Like it or not, Ray, you made an agreement with your wife about a very serious issue. I commend you for discussing and resolving the question before the marriage. Grace went into the marriage and the baby with the assumption that the religious issue had been settled—and it has. That doesn't mean you can't expose your son to other religious traditions, but it does mean that you must honor your agreement with your wife, and try to do it without creating a permanent rift between your parents and your wife.

# Congratulations: You're a Dad!

Ready or not, guys, you're going to risk fatherhood if you engage in sex. Even birth control isn't foolproof.

EDWARD: Sue and I dated for about six months. I also dated other women, and she knew it. Last week she told me she's pregnant. She's twenty-four and has a good job. She always assured me she was using birth control, so I was shocked when she dropped this bombshell. I'm not even sure the baby is mine. She wants me to help her out financially through her pregnancy and, of course, support the child. I think this is totally unfair.

SUE: I am hurt that Edward would even suggest he's not the father. He knows he's the only one I

have been intimate with for a long time. And
while I did know he was seeing other people,
he always told me that I was the special one. I
believed him. I didn't make this baby alone,
and he should do the right thing.

## Judge Judy Says:

First things first, Edward. The law doesn't care whether
you said, "I love you," whether you said, "I do," whether
you said, "I promise to take care of you." The law doesn't
give a rat's behind about that. The law says the child is an
innocent, and the child has the right to be supported by
both parents, whether they are happy parents or unhappy
parents. I understand your angst, because this was not
something you wanted or planned. However, you did have
some complicity in the conception, if it is in fact your
child. I hope you'll take this as a lesson that each individ-
ual is responsible for birth control. Now, you say you
aren't sure that it's your child. You'll have to wait until after the child is born to determine that through DNA testing, which is foolproof. Once that's done, you will know
what your responsibilities are. Just in case she's right and
this is your child, I'd start saving now.

**Congratulations: You're a Dad!**

# Ah, Foolish Youth

Sometimes I think that the greatest invention of the new millennium would be a mechanism to delay puberty until age twenty-one. That means you could order a drink and become a parent in the same year.

MADDIE:   Our nineteen-year-old son, Patrick, attends school in another city. He just informed us that he and a woman he met on a school break in Florida are going to have a baby. She works in a bar, and it seems they went out (or, rather, *in*) two or three times when he was on vacation. She called him at school last night and informed him that she's pregnant. Now, this moron that I have raised says he must do the right thing and marry her so that the child won't be illegitimate. That's preposterous, even if the child is his, which is open to question. We've tried talking to him, but he won't listen.

PATRICK:   I can't understand my parents. They always taught me to take responsibility for myself. This woman wouldn't lie to me about something so important as being the father of her baby. I must do the right thing. I fathered a child and must marry her. I can finish school at night and work during the day.

## Judge Judy Says:

Listen to your mother, birdbrain. What she's saying is first wait and be sure. If the child is yours, you must surely be responsible and contribute to its support, both financial and emotional. It would not, however, necessarily be responsible to marry a woman you hardly know. You've already made one mistake by not keeping your pants zipped. Don't make another.

# 5

# After the Ball Is Over

## (Don't get mad. Get out. Move on.)

Divorce is always a complicated affair. As a lawyer and later as a judge, I saw divorcing couples waste their most productive years litigating over trivia. I tried to convince them to put a period to their failed marriages as quickly as possible, to make concessions and get on with the business of living. Unfortunately, it often didn't work. Many divorcing couples are more interested in punishing than living.

## Dividing the Goods

What happens when parents make a substantial gift to their married children, and then divorce happens?

MARY:   My husband of fifteen years and I are
        divorcing. We have two children. Eight years
        ago, my parents gave us $50,000 as a down
        payment on our first home. The children and I
        are staying in the home, and my husband
        insists that he is entitled to half the equity in
        the house. I think that $50,000 should be
        deducted, as it was a gift from my parents.

DOUG:   The $50,000 was a gift to both of us. And
        since we are dividing all of our assets, the
        $50,000 should be divided just like everything
        else.

## Judge Judy Says:

From a legal perspective, since the house is in both of
your names, the equity in the house belongs equally to
both of you, if you are dividing your property fifty-fifty.
My advice to parents who give their married children a
substantial gift for the purchase of a house is to have a
contract in writing stipulating that should your children
divorce and sell the house, the money you gave them
must be returned to you and not be included as joint
property. You can always change your mind later, but
make your intentions clear from the beginning.

# My Friends, My Gifts

Or, whose gift was it, anyway?

GINNIE:    My soon-to-be ex-husband and I have been
           married for less than a year. We had a large
           wedding. Most of the guests were my family
           and friends. Jeff has a small family, and with
           his personality, no friends. We are in the
           process of trying to settle property. I believe
           that all the gifts from my family and friends
           should be mine. He can keep the two picture
           frames, the salt and pepper shakers, and the
           bun warmer from his clan.

JEFF:      Excuse me, but I thought that when a gift was
           given to a couple it became joint property.
           Something is not right with this picture. She
           keeps the ring. She keeps the furniture, the
           TV, the stereo, and the china. I keep the
           memories and my cat.

## Judge Judy Says:

The gifts were given to you as a couple, and they became
joint property to be divided equally. The division should
be based on the value of the gifts, not who gave them.
That's my legal response. However, I also urge you to be

smart. Try to make the division of property as amicable as possible, otherwise the only ones to profit will be the lawyers. From the perspective of what's right, I think if Jenny's aunt gave her a set of flatware, Jenny should keep it. If Jenny's parents gave crystal, then she should keep it. Jeff, if what you and your family contributed to this short-term blink-of-an-eye marriage was two picture frames and a cat, that is what you should take with you.

# Who Keeps the Friends?

After you get through with who keeps the china and the ballet subscription, what happens to the formerly mutual friends?

ARLENE:   My husband, Larry, and I have been close friends with Sherry and Mike for fifteen years. We vacationed together, and our kids grew up together. Now Mike has left Sherry and is living with another woman. Sherry is devastated. It has been a terrible situation for all of us. Well, last week Larry ran into Mike at the market, and they discussed going out to dinner—the four of us. Just like old times, right? Except that the fourth person in this

cozy group is the woman Mike left Sherry for.
I speak to Sherry daily, and as far as I'm
concerned, this would be an act of betrayal.
What is Larry thinking?

LARRY:   Mike is my friend. I'm not going to cut him
off. Besides, he's really serious about this
woman, and in time, I expect Sherry will find
someone new. When she does, I'll have
absolutely no problem going out with her and
her new man. Besides, this isn't a big deal. It's
only dinner.

## Judge Judy Says:

When a divorce is contentious, it's not unusual for
friends to take different sides, at least in the beginning.
There are some fresh wounds here, Larry, and you have
to understand that. If you're lucky, with time you'll be
able to maintain friendships with both parties—although
that requires a combination of maturity and understanding that many people can't manage. For now, Larry, don't
try to force a foursome. Maintain your friendship with
Mike. Have lunch with him. Play golf. Talk. Let some
healing occur before you suggest more.

# Get Out and On with It

A divorce can be easy, or a divorce can be hard. It's your choice.

EDDIE:    After four years of marriage—three of them miserable—Claire and I are divorcing. Thankfully, we have no children. Claire is a social worker, and she has a good job. I work in a family business with my dad and brother. Now Claire's saying she wants a cut of the business as part of the settlement. I say she's crazy.

CLAIRE:    Eddie isn't telling you the whole story. It's true that we were legally married for four years, but we've been together for twelve. It took him eight years to propose. I, like a fool, hung in there and waited. So much for the value of a long courtship in predicting the success of a marriage. Anyway, after twelve years of being a couple, why should I walk away with nothing?

## Judge Judy Says:

Claire, the length of the courtship should have been a clue that Eddie wouldn't take too well to marriage. However, it was your choice to wait around. The fact remains, you had a short-term marriage. You deserve a brief period of additional support to allow you to regroup—not a lifetime annuity.

# Whither Sparky?

For some divorcing couples, the custody fight over a beloved pet is fierce. There are no truly right answers, but a little maturity and a dose of perspective help.

NATALIE:   When Avery and I got married, within the first six months, we bought a beautiful little dog—a Cavalier King Charles Spaniel. We both loved Sparky to death. He slept with us, he traveled with us. We adored him. However, we came not to adore each other. Within two years we had decided to separate. Avery moved into his own place. I stayed in our apartment. We didn't want our separation to be traumatic for Sparky, so we made an arrangement. He would live with me during the week, and Avery could take him for visitation on the weekends. It worked out very well until I met Paul. Paul and I became engaged three months ago, and we are planning to marry. Every Friday when Avery comes to pick up Sparky, Paul throws a fit. He says it's not as if Avery is picking up his children. It's a dog. Paul wonders if Avery is going to be in our lives for the next ten or fifteen years or as long as Sparky is living. It has reached the point where we spend half of our weekends arguing about the dog. I've broached the subject with Avery about him moving on with his life, which includes getting a new dog, and he won't hear of it.

AVERY:   Sparky is a member of the family. Pets aren't fungible, neither are children. If we had kids, would Natalie tell me to just get a new kid? I have a relationship with Sparky. Paul's being a jerk about it.

## Judge Judy Says:

This is a very tough question. I love my dog, so I know what that feels like. However, let's be honest. It seems to me that Sparky would not suffer one iota if left in Natalie's care permanently. Avery, you would suffer for a while, but surely you must see that this arrangement can't continue. From an emotional standpoint, it's not good for the three of you to continue to have regular contact with each other. Certainly this new marriage is not going to thrive with Sparky being shuttled back and forth every weekend. Avery, it's time for you to seek a new companion.

# 6

# Tug-of-Wars

## (Love your kids more than you hate each other.)

My father once said to me when I was contemplating divorce from my first husband, "Two innocent people shouldn't suffer for what two guilty people did." That is damn good advice for divorcing couples with children. Once the decision to divorce has been made, all other decisions must revolve around one single objective—the long- and short-term best interests of the children. Love your kids more than you hate each other.

## His Women du Jour

When parents divorce, there's a good chance that the children will spend part of their childhood exposed to new significant others. How parents deal with the introduction of new people should be guided by the comfort of the kids, at least in the beginning, especially with young children who are the most vulnerable and confused. That's a lesson Sharon and Bill might take to heart.

SHARON: Every other Saturday morning Bill, my ex, picks up the kids for visitation, but he never comes alone. He always brings a weekend date *du jour*. It really rankles me. Believe me when I say that it's never the same woman twice. I wouldn't be so upset, but sometimes the kids complain to me that he pays more attention to his date than he does to them. When I try to broach the subject, he tells me to get a life and not give him orders.

BILL: This is the real-life world. I'm single, I date. Why should I alter what is natural just because she can't stand that I'm moving on with my life?

## Judge Judy Says:

There's only one question here: What's best for the kids? Everything else is secondary. They did not choose for you to marry, give birth to them, then divorce. It's right for you to move on with your life, Bill, but the children's emotional security must be your first priority. Frankly, I could never understand why a man would insist on combining a date with his children's visitation when he could just as easily have the date any other day of the week. Bill, ask yourself why you're afraid to be alone with your children.

On the other hand, Sharon, be honest. Does it bother the kids, or does it just irritate you? If you're the only one who's complaining, deal with it like an adult. Bottom line for both of you: Ask the kids how they feel and be guided by what they say.

# Riches to Rags

When divorced parents have a disagreement involving the children, they really have to ask themselves whether it's a legitimate issue or whether they're just trying to bust each other's chops.

SYLVIA:    Phil and I have been divorced for two years,
           separated for three. We have two children,
           ages eight and nine, and they go with their
           father on the weekends. Since our separation,
           each visitation has been turned into a war, and
           I am at my wits' end. I send the kids with nice,
           clean clothes, nothing torn, everything fresh.

Phil brings them home unwashed, with filthy clothes, ripped at the knees. I've considered sending them in rags, but that's not fair to the kids. It seems to me that Phil should buy some extra things to keep at his house. He should return the kids the way I sent them. I'm not his maid anymore.

PHIL:    This is typical of Sylvia's obsessive-compulsive behavior. The important thing is, the kids and I have a great time on the weekends. Why do they have to preen themselves in order to go home?

## Judge Judy Says:

Repeat this mantra: *It's not about me, it's not about me, it's not about me.* Sylvia, your kids are benefiting by having fun with their dad. If they are out for the day, it's ridiculous for them to cut short activities to shower and change before they come home. On the other hand, Phil, you should replace anything torn or ruined on your watch. Work it out with the kids in mind.

# Transient Kids, Permanent Toys

These proprietary battles divorced parents have really burn me up. It's obvious that the arguments are not about doing what's best for the children. Quite to the contrary. I've heard it all. If it's not about clothes, it's about toys. One so-called adult divorced male pulled the following stunt: His four-year-old son visited him one weekend a month and over the holidays. Dad gave him the toy he'd been longing for at Christmas, then informed him that the toy could not be taken home to Mom's but only played with at Dad's once a month. The poor kid didn't understand, and he was bereft when he couldn't have his toy at the end of the visit. The following scenario is just another variation on that theme.

MARY:   Jack and I have been divorced for a year, and our son, Tommy, is eleven. He visits with his father two weekends a month. I work full-time, and neither one of us has a great deal of money or has remarried. Jack bought Tommy a computer for Christmas, but the computer stays at his house, so Tommy can only use it two weekends a month. If Tommy needs to use it for school or just wants to fool around with it during the rest of the month, he's out of luck. Jack and I have had a big argument over it, because I feel that the computer should be at home where Tommy can use it all the time.

JACK:   I paid for it, so it stays at my house. If Mary wants to buy the kid a computer for her house, she's welcome to do it. But I'm certainly not just handing over an expensive piece of equipment.

## Judge Judy Says:

I've heard both sides. Now what I want to know is what Tommy has to say about this. So far we've covered each of your egos, especially Dad's, but we haven't talked about what is in the best interests of your child. It would seem to me that Tommy's best interests would be served by having that computer available to him all the time when he needs to do his homework, when he needs to write a report, or for whatever reason. Jack, keeping the computer at your house is like dangling a carrot in front of Tommy to make your house a more appealing place than his mom's. That is not in his best interests, is it? It's purely for your ego. Stop playing these games and do the right thing. Your son won't be a child forever. He will eventually understand that you are a manipulative jackass.

# Show Up and Grow Up

It's hard to be a kid when your parents aren't adults.

SHAWN:    My ex-husband, Chris, can't get his act
          together when it comes to visitation. He

**Show Up and Grow Up**

doesn't show up. He shows up too late. He switches dates at the last minute. He was irresponsible when we were married, and he's continuing that irresponsible behavior. It's so unfair to the children. It's unfair to me, too, because I can't make plans of my own. I've told Chris that unless he adheres to the order of the visitation that was made by the court, I'm going to cut off the visits.

CHRIS: I'm doing the best I can. I have work commitments. I have social commitments. I have a life, too. I play softball, and sometimes a game is rained out on Saturday. If they reschedule it for Sunday, what's the big deal if I call and say I'll pick up the kids on Saturday instead?

## Judge Judy Says:

What's the big deal? Let's start with a basic fact: Children thrive on structure. The security of routine is what makes them comfortable. Their lives have already been turned upside down by the divorce of two people whom they love. It seems to me if you have to forgo an obligation in order not to disappoint your children, that's what a responsible parent does. You think of your children first. And here's a reality check for you: If you can't accomplish this with your own internal controls, Shawn would be within her rights to ask a family court judge to fix a more structured order of visitation. That would put you on a legal tether, and require that you give seventy-two hours notice or miss the visitation.

# Whose Visitation Is It?

I used to tell women who insisted on limiting and micromanaging their ex's visitation that they were being spiteful and stupid. They were depriving themselves of some quiet private time, and their children would come to resent them in time. Hannah is typical.

HANNAH:   I think it's very important for the kids to spend
            good quality time with their father on the
            weekends. The problem is that Ben routinely
            picks up the children Saturday morning,
            proceeds to deposit them with his parents,
            and takes off to do chores, see friends,
            whatever. Comes back, takes them out to
            dinner, watches a little television, and brings
            them home. The children tell me they spend a
            lovely afternoon with their grandparents but
            see very little of their father. I told him that
            unless he spends time with his children there

is no need for him to pick them up on
Saturdays.

BEN:      It seems to me that their grandparents are a
very important part of my children's life. My
children love them and they love to visit with
my children. Saturday is the only day that I
have not only to see my children, but to do all
my chores, because I work six days a week.
Right now I'm working two jobs to take care of
my child support obligations and live myself,
so why is Hannah busting my chops about
this? What does she want from me?

## Judge Judy Says:

Hannah, I have a question for you: Who's complaining?
You or the kids? The only time that this should be an issue is if the children are complaining that they are not
enjoying their Saturdays and feel that their father is ne-
glecting them. Children usually love to spend time with
their grandparents. They love to be spoiled and showered
with affection. So, Hannah, if your children aren't unhappy, stop worrying. Take the day for yourself. Go out.
Get a manicure. Get a pedicure. Get a facial. Get a mas-
sage. Go shopping in a mall. Have lunch with a friend.
Take advantage of the day. As for you, Ben, it sounds as if
you could use a dose of maturity, even though I agree

**Whose Visitation Is It?**

with your position. You're missing the only opportunity you have to be involved with your children, and you will regret that someday.

# Visitation by the Book

Children of divorce always get the short end of the stick when the couple engages in a bitter battle. Sadly, when parents are in a rage against each other, they lack objectivity about the children's needs. They don't see how their behavior may be hurting the children. Years later, when they lament, "I don't know what went wrong with Junior," they fail to see that what went wrong was how they handled their separation and divorce.

ROBERT:    When June and I married, she had a two-year-old child from a previous relationship. The following year we had a child together. I was like a father to Scotty, since he never knew his real father. Unfortunately, our marriage fell apart after six years. June is very angry. I want to take both children on my weekend visits. June says I can only take our biological child, not Scotty. This is devastating to me, and also to my parents, who love Scotty as if he were their own grandchild.

**Visitation by the Book**

JUNE:   He's such a lying bastard. I can hardly bear to
        see him when he comes to pick up Charlie,
        our child, no less giving him the satisfaction of
        being able to be the poster boy of a good
        father and pick up both children. I don't care
        if he's unhappy, and I don't care if his parents
        are unhappy. He had an affair with my best
        friend for more than a year. I returned one day
        from visiting my folks and found them in my
        home together. She just left her husband, and
        they're planning to marry as soon as that
        divorce is final. Some father.

## Judge Judy Says:

June, you're 100 percent right about one thing: The guy
is a putz. But you picked him, so he's your putz. You
brought him into your son's life, and it would be terribly
unfair to your boy to cut him off from the only father he
knows. Even if the law gives you that right, it doesn't
make it *right*. When you introduce a father figure into
your child's life, that child's emotions are not turned off
simultaneously with yours. It's not about you, honey, it's
about your son.

# A Question of Control

I've always found it so sad that children of divorce often lose touch with half of their family, aunts, uncles, sometimes even grandparents, almost always their cousins. Everyone should work to ensure that children of divorced parents are not deprived of a family as well.

EVELYN: Sam and I have a problem. Sam's brother Mark and his wife Barbara are divorced. They have two children, whom we adore. Mark sees the children every second Sunday. We still have a very pleasant relationship with Barbara, and our kids are very close. We called Barbara and invited the children for a sleepover with our kids, which they used to do all the time. Sam's brother got wind of this call and was furious. He said that any plans we make with his children must go through him. If we want to have the children over, it will have to be on the day that he has visitation, and to go through Barbara is like stabbing him in the back.

MARK: Look, this is tough enough. I at least want to feel as if my family is supporting me and not going behind my back to my ex-wife. We've been battling over custody and visitation and money for the last year. We do not have a good relationship, and I'd like to feel that at least I have some control over my children when it comes to my own family.

## Judge Judy Says:

Mark, it's easy to see why your court battles over custody and money have been so prolonged. That's what happens when parents put themselves before their children. Your brother and sister-in-law are not only right, but they seem to be more concerned about your children's best interests than you are. Certainly, what you suggest is cutting off cousins who have been close and relegating them to every second Sunday, if that. What skin is it off your nose if arrangements are made through your former wife for the benefit of your children? Grow up.

# Badmouthing

Jennifer is an eleven-year-old girl who lives with her mother. Her parents went through a very bitter divorce, and Jennifer feels caught in the middle. Her mother doesn't realize how much it hurts Jennifer when she overhears her saying mean things about Dad, whom Jennifer adores. When you indulge your hostility by speaking disparagingly about your ex within earshot of your children, you make yourself feel better and the kids feel lousy. The choice should be simple, but some adults don't get it. In the end, your children will hate you for it—and you'll deserve it.

JENNIFER: My mom is always saying bad things about my dad on the phone when she's talking to her friends and Grandma. I told her I don't like it. It makes me unhappy when I hear her saying some of those things. She says if I don't like it I should go in another room, but even when I don't hear her, I know she's doing it.

MOM: I never say anything derogatory about my former husband to my daughter. But I'm a person too, and I need to vent. If I don't tell someone about the hell that Jennifer's father is putting me through, I'll explode. So I talk to my mother or my friends on the phone. I never purposely do it while Jennifer is in the room, but sometimes she'll walk in when I'm in the middle of a conversation. I think she listens on purpose, if you want the truth. If she doesn't like what I'm saying, she should shut the door of her room.

## Judge Judy Says:

You're 150 percent wrong, lady. Nothing, I repeat, *nothing* is private when there is an eleven-year-old girl within earshot. Your conversations disturb your daughter, and since her happiness should be your priority, save your private kvetching conversations for when she's at school or outside. Jennifer sounds like a pretty smart kid to me. She not only hears something that she's not supposed to hear, but she's articulated to you that it makes her feel awful. Hearing bad things said about a parent, especially from another parent, does not make a child feel good about herself. It makes her feel badly about herself. Ultimately, she will resent, not the father whom you are maligning, but you, the maligner.

# Pick Your Battleground

. . . and that should never, ever be in front of or within earshot of your children, period. End of discussion. But Charlene just didn't get it.

CHARLENE: My ex and I have been divorced for a year, and we don't communicate. He's always late with support, and the only time I can talk to him is when he comes to pick up the kids for visitation. It always turns into an ugly scene, and he is taking me back to court to change the place where we pick up the children. He says he won't put them in the middle of our arguments. Let him get his support payments in on time, and there wouldn't be a problem.

CHARLES: I send my support through the court. I pay on time. The court sometimes delays getting the payments out. Charlene would like me to pay her directly. We tried that, and there were always arguments. Now the court takes care of it, and I am protected. The kids should not be involved in this nuttiness when she sees me.

## Judge Judy Says:

Never discuss finances around children. Period. As far as the payments are concerned, Charles is right. He may get his check to the court on time, and it's the court's delay, not his. Remember, the court is a bureaucracy. The people processing these checks are all over the place. One goes on vacation, one is taking his comp day, one has a nurturing day, one is out for a week—and sometimes the check is delayed. Charlene, if you *really* want to be irritated, you can take it up with the court, but I warn you, it won't do any good. My advice is to budget accordingly, knowing that the check is going to have a week's lag.

# Little Spies

Never make children co-conspirators in your nuttiness.

CALLIE:    I am seven years old. When I visit with my
           dad, he's always asking questions about my
           mom. And Mom is always asking questions
           about him, too. I don't like it. They each want
           to know about who visits when I'm home, and
           if anyone sleeps over. They also want me to tell
           them about any new things in the house. Then
           they tell me not to say they asked. It makes me
           sad.

MOM:       I think it's very important for parents to know
           what's going on in the homes where their
           children are living and visiting. I want to make
           sure that my child is being well taken care of
           when she's with her father. What's she eating?
           Who's preparing the meals? Where are they
           going at night? Whether her dad is spending
           hours on the phone instead of paying attention
           to her. Whether he's drinking any alcohol,
           which used to be a problem. I hate to make
           Callie uncomfortable, but this is my
           responsibility as her mother.

DAD:       And it's my responsibility as her father to find
           out whether my former wife has a parade of

**Little Spies**

men coming in and out of the house. Is my
daughter seeing a new guy every other
Thursday when she comes out of her room?
My former wife isn't going to tell me that. My
child has to tell me that.

## Judge Judy Says:

Whew! Such hostility in the guise of caring for your
daughter! Your true concerns are quite transparent. Both
of you should run, don't walk, but run and sign up for a
course in Child Rearing 101. The first thing that any psy-
chiatrist, psychologist, educator, or therapist will tell you
is that you never put a child in the position of being a spy
for the other parent. It makes that child feel horrible—and
also reinforces the misconception children have that they
are somehow to blame for their parents' divorce. If you're
so interested in finding out what is going on under the
sheets in your former mate's house, hire a private investigator. But make sure that private investigator is at least
postpubescent.

# The Grandparents' Dilemma

Grandparents are very important for children, and, believe me, vice versa. To have skipped over the children

and just have the grandchildren would be the ultimate paradise. In divorces, there can be an alienation that is deeply painful. In the following scenarios, loving grandparents wrestle with the consequences of their childrens' divorces. Do grandparents have legal rights?

# The Wayward Son

SAM AND LOUISE: To put it bluntly, our thirty-one-year-old son is a bum. We have modest means, but we do try to help out financially. We've continued to help support our son's ex-wife and our grandchildren, whom we adore. Now our ex-daughter-in-law has remarried a Navy man and plans on relocating across the country. We are devastated. Can we stop her from taking our grandchildren so far away?

KAREN: I adore my former in-laws. How they could have raised such a son leads me to believe that there were babies switched at birth. However, I found a wonderful man who is supportive of me and treats the children like a real dad should. His job takes us to a new place and a new start. How can they prevent me from moving?

## Judge Judy Says:

While legally there is nothing grandparents can do to prevent your remarriage and relocation, I strongly urge that it is in the best interests of the children that you make specific plans to have the kids visit with their grandparents several times a year. Children thrive on the widest community of love and support. Grandparents are usually the best example of nonparental love. Don't deny the kids.

# Only What's Best

While I never underestimate the value of grandmas and grandpas, I am quick to point out that it is the parents' right to bring up their children, unless they are abusive or neglectful, which is certainly not the case in the story that follows.

EDNA:    Our beautiful daughter died, leaving a
         husband and two children, a boy three and a
         girl six. I'm a fifty-six-year-old retired
         schoolteacher. Our son-in-law is a well-
         intentioned, hardworking salesman who has
         put our grandson in a day care center and
         arranged for neighbors to babysit with the kids
         when he's working. We believe that the kids

would be better off with us. We are well off
financially, and could be with the kids all the
time.

HAL:    Her parents told me that I should allow them
to raise our children, that it was cruel for the
kids to be left with strangers while I work. I
have been a good husband and father. I know
it will be difficult for me and hard for the kids,
but I love them, and I don't want to lose them.
My in-laws have threatened to fight for
custody. What should I do?

## Judge Judy Says:

Edna, you're way out of line and would surely lose the
custody battle. Hal needs your help and support. His
children probably need him now more than ever. Be good
grandparents. Help out. Be available on his terms.

# Mixed Motivations

Sadly, children are too often used as a means of seeking
revenge.

CAROL:   When my husband was killed, we were all
devastated. My in-laws were supportive, until

they discovered my husband had left me a one-quarter interest in the family business. There are hard feelings. When I remarried and relocated, I decided that my boys would be less stressed if we severed ties with my in-laws. They're planning to fight me in court. Don't I have a right to decide who my children visit?

ALAN AND SARAH: There were no hard feelings when Carol inherited a piece of the family business. The acrimony developed when she threatened to sell to a stranger unless we hired a new president who knew nothing about the business, or anything else, for that matter. We love our grandchildren and intend to fight to see them if we want.

## Judge Judy Says:

In many states, grandparents do have the right to petition for visitation. The fight is usually a bloodbath in which everybody loses. Put your personal feelings aside and carve out a Sunday each month for the kids to be loved up by Grandma and Grandpa. In the years to come, the children will thank you.

# 7

# The Second Time
# Around

(For better or forget about it.)

When I married Jerry, I quipped at the ceremony, "For better . . . or forget it." I was only half kidding. Most people view "the second time around" as a fresh opportunity—a chance to learn from the mistakes of the past and to finally get it right. But the second time around is hardly the proverbial clean slate for most people. They've got baggage—children and exes and debts and other complications. Taking a chance on a new commitment may be a good thing, but you have to go into it with your eyes wide open.

# Ex-Entanglements

In a perfect world, a parent wouldn't be wooing a new lover while his children from a failed love match stood by and gawked.

PRESLEY:    Ginny and I have been divorced for five years. We have two children together, and I see the children every weekend from Friday to Sunday. Six months ago I met a woman I'm very serious about. She has moved in with me. Now Ginny says that as long as we are sharing a bedroom, she will not permit the children to come over and spend the night. She is actually threatening to take me back to court.

GINNY:    I'm trying to raise my children to be moral people, in spite of Presley. Having premarital sex is not something I want my children to think is okay. The kids know they're not married, and I think it's wrong. Unless Presley and his live-in consent to not sharing a bedroom while my children are visiting, I intend to go to court. By the way, I date, too, but I don't have my male friends stay over in the house. Besides, my ex has five nights a week to share a bed with his girlfriend.

## Judge Judy Says:

Whatever Ginny's motivations may be, Presley, the children are bound to find themselves in the middle and feeling very uncomfortable. Think "children first." In the big picture, we're not talking about an enormous sacrifice here. Ask yourself what message you want your children to take away about your new relationship. Remember, someday they're going to be teenagers and you'll need to be able to speak with the voice of moral authority. Don't blow your chance.

# Second-Class Children

Blended families require extra-special effort. Jerry and I each brought young children into our marriage. Twenty-plus years later, they are close friends who all consider themselves siblings. Nothing gives us more joy or sense of accomplishment, but it didn't happen automatically or overnight. We both made some mistakes. Balancing a new marriage with the needs of children already traumatized by divorce creates conflict. Making the children of blended families feel secure and treated equally is a big parenting challenge. Kids have exquisitely sensitive radar for any sign of unfairness, and you have to bend over backwards to make sure they don't feel shortchanged.

ELLIS:      It is a second marriage for both Gail and me,
            and we each have children living with us. My
            boys are twelve and fourteen. Gail has a seven-
            year-old boy and a six-year-old girl. Gail has a
            three-bedroom house, and we are planning to
            fix up the basement for my two boys. When we
            told them, they were angry about being
            relegated to the basement.

THE BOYS, JOE AND NED: If we're all going to be part of
            the family, we should be treated like equals. If
            they're going to fix something up, why don't
            they have Gail's two kids bunk in one room,
            and we'll have one room? And if they want to
            fix up the basement as a playroom or as a
            common room so we all have a little extra
            space, that would be great. We don't want to
            be put in the basement.

## Judge Judy Says:

If the boys are unhappy about being relegated to the
basement, believe me, that will change in time. As they
get a little older, they will love having their private space
down there far away from the watchful eyes and ears of
their parents. At this point, since it's a new relationship
and the boys feel strongly that they don't want to be put
in the basement, double up the six- and seven-year-old

for a while and put the boys together, so that you're all on the same level. Of course, you might be very, very smart and fix up a suite for yourselves in the basement that would be quite private. Frankly, this would be my first choice as a newlywed.

# Drop the Grudge

The definition of "family" is not only blood relatives. The people who constitute your family are those who perform that role in your life. George thought he could just walk away without causing pain. He just didn't get it.

BARBARA:  I am a reasonably together thirty-year-old single professional woman. My parents divorced when I was five. Mom remarried and I adored my stepfather for the ten years they were together until their divorce. I thought he loved me, but after the divorce he cut us all off. Even though five years have passed, I finally reached out to him. He was cordial, but he doesn't really want to see me. I feel so rejected.

GEORGE:  Barbara and I were like father and daughter for ten years. I had no other children and lavished all my attention on her. The divorce from her mother was not pleasant, and I was disappointed when Barbara refused to take a neutral position. Instead, she sided with her mother. I just felt it was best to get on with my life. She made her choice.

## Judge Judy Says:

George, your divorce was between you and Barbara's mother. It's not fair to place the burden on Barbara. Even adult children—maybe especially adult children—have a difficult time when their parents divorce. You claim to have loved her like your own, and now she's reaching out to you. You'll always regret it if you don't accept this gesture of reconciliation.

# A May-December Dilemma

In the first flush of love, people have a hard time getting real. But there are some inevitable realities when a man marries a woman twenty years his junior—as Fred discovered.

FRED:    I am a fifty-seven-year-old successful lawyer. Divorced eight years, with three adult children. I met and fell in love with Ilyana, a thirty-year-old social worker. Our relationship is perfect. We are so compatible. We enjoy the same things, we love to travel, and we have a terrific circle of friends. Obviously, we talked about children before we were married. I told Ilyana straight out that I didn't want more, and she assured me that she didn't want children either. Now that we're married for three years, she is pressuring me to have a child. She says it's unfair to hold her to her previous position when she was happy without children, but I think she's the one who's being unfair. I was honest with her about what I wanted, and now she's trying to change the rules.

ILYANA: What can I say? My feelings changed. I didn't plan on it, but it happened. I want Fred's baby. I want us to make something lasting together. I didn't realize how important it would be for me to have a family, and I don't think it's fair to hold me to that agreement. Fred is older. What happens if he dies and I'm left all alone? At least if I had a child, I would have a family.

## Judge Judy Says:

Fred, Fred, Fred—get real. If you're a fifty-seven-year-old man and you marry a thirty-year-old woman, the chances are that she is going to want to have a child sooner or later. I don't care what she said three years ago. So you have to be smart here, even if you weren't being smart before you got married. If you say no to children, you will be creating a rift that you will never be able to overcome in your marriage. She will resent you, and that resentment will manifest itself from the breakfast room to the bedroom. That's your choice. Make it carefully.

# Reality Check

Couples have to use their heads—before the wedding day. They have to give some thought to what is likely to happen in a marriage, given the ages and circumstances. If you're twenty-eight and you marry a forty-five-year-old guy with a couple of kids, you can kiss those long intimate weekends goodbye. It's just a fact.

SYLVIA:   I am twenty-eight years old and newly married to Evan, who is forty-five. He has three children from his first marriage. I have none. We knew each other eight months before we married. During that time, we spent at least two weekends a month alone. Now that we are married, his ex-wife uses us as a baby-sitting service. It seems like she's always off

TORE

**Reality Check**

somewhere, and the kids are with us. They're great children, but this is a new marriage, and we need some time alone. My husband just can't say no to her, and it's causing all sorts of arguments.

EVAN:   Sylvia knew I had children, and I love being with them. My ex has finally agreed to more liberal visitation, and I have every intention of taking advantage of it.

## Judge Judy Says:

Sylvia, if you marry a man with kids, don't expect to have romantic weekends alone in the Bahamas. If you are a good partner, you will understand that being a weekend father carries with it a measure of guilt about not being there full-time. Be supportive from the heart. It will make both of you and the kids feel great.

# Love Me, Love My Kids

We've all heard the stories of the new love who declares he's "not a child person." But there the kids are. You know what I mean. The divorced mom falls madly in love with her ski instructor, who's all macho man and fun, but not much of a parental figure. He says, "I love you, and I understand you have kids. I'll live with them, but they're not gonna be my responsibility." Is that the kind of man a good mother wants to bring into her house? More often than not, these kinds of relationships are fraught with disaster. Be very careful—and keep your ears open—as Cathy needs to do when Jerry tells her how he really feels.

JERRY:    My kids are grown, but Cathy still has a sixteen-year-old living at home. Cathy and I are very much in love, but frankly, the kid is a problem for me. I already raised my children. I really don't want to be involved in the day-to-day raising of a teenager. I'd rather put off the wedding and moving in together until Jason is out of high school and off to college. Cathy doesn't understand at all.

CATHY:    I *don't* understand. It's not as if Jerry isn't a parent. Besides, Jason's a good kid. He has teenage problems, but nothing serious. I wonder if Jerry is getting cold feet about marrying me and that's what this is about. I'm ready to lay down the law and demand that we set a date.

## Judge Judy Says:

Cathy, it sounds to me as if Jerry is being honest and up front, and you don't want to hear it. Simply put,

Jerry feels that he's done his duty as a parent. He likes Jason—he just doesn't want to live with him. Why create a strained living arrangement from the get-go? Back off and enjoy this romantic time. It could be the best of times—spend an occasional weekend away together, or steal a night or two when Jason's off to a friend's house. Raising a teenager is difficult enough. Doing it with a reluctant spouse is nuts.

# A Special Place in Hell

There should be a special place in hell for parents who divorce, remarry, and forget the children they created the first time around. You get the feeling they're thinking, "That's my old, *imperfect* family, and this is my new, *perfect* family." That is, until a possible third, *more perfect* family comes along. More often than not, it is the fathers who walk away from the first family and start a second. It's beyond me why people feel as if they have a license to go out and create a second family that they cannot afford emotionally or financially, leaving their first family in a state of near abandonment.

PAULA:    Stan and I were married for six years, and we have two children, a boy and a girl. We've been divorced for four years. Three years ago, Stan remarried, and he and his wife have twin daughters. Although Stan pays child support, he has essentially deserted our children. He rarely sees them or calls them. Of course, they're extremely hurt, and I don't know how to put a nice spin on it. The truth is, our kids have been replaced.

STAN: Unfortunately, Paula doesn't understand that I only have one behind. I try to do the right thing, but I now have a second family with young children. I hold down a full-time job and a part-time job to help pay child support to Paula, as well as taking care of my present family. What does she want from me? I do my best.

## Judge Judy Says:

Your best ain't good enough, Stan. People who elect to have second families should do so with something in the back of their head saying to them, "Can you manage all of this and still be a good father to your first family?" If you need more than one behind to take care of your two families, then I suggest you start pumping up. There are some animals that can walk away from their children, but human beings are not supposed to be able to.

# Reach Out and Touch Someone Else

You are one of those civilized divorced families who celebrates birthdays, graduations, and anniversaries together, for the sake of your children. Maintaining a friendly, cordial, respectful relationship with your ex is always good. But sometimes one party just hates to let go and hangs on to a life that no longer exists.

RUTH:   I like to talk to my ex on the phone. We have a decent relationship, and it's important that we stay connected for the sake of the children. I tell Joel what's happening in their lives, and I know he appreciates these daily updates. Well, lately when I call to report on the kids, he is very distant and all business. I know what's going on. Eva, his new wife, laid down the law. Eva is going to have to come to terms with the connection that we will always have as parents, and Joel should have the guts to tell her so rather than shut me out.

JOEL:   Here I am caught between a rock and a hard place. Ruth calls at least two or three times a week to tell me about the children. I am grateful that we have a reasonable relationship, but all I have to do is ask her, "How are you?" and she can go on for a one-hour monologue. Eva gets nuts. She says I would get nuts, too, if her former fiancé checked in once a week and she schmoozed with him for an hour. I think this is different.

EVA: When I married Joel, I clearly understood that he had two kids and an ex, and that because the kids were young (eight and ten), he and Ruth would need to keep the lines of communication open. I have no problem with that. I don't think I'm being unreasonable when I say that it's irritating for them to have these hour-long phone conversations about the kids' visits with their maternal grandparents, and about what the kids are eating and who they're playing with, and Ruth's social life. My sense is that the former Mrs. is trying to maintain that thread of a relationship with my husband through the children.

## Judge Judy Says:

Joel, you are taking the path of least resistance—which happens to be the wrong choice. Find out about the children from the children. Speak to the children every day about what they're doing and what their days are like.

Conversations between you and Ruth should be friendly, but brief. I agree with you, Eva, that it is not only unhealthy for you and your husband, but also unhealthy for Ruth to try to maintain the semblance of family beyond the children. Ruth, it's time for you to seek new adult companionship.

# They Call Her Mommy

Divorce and remarriage can cause enough complications without adding unnecessary issues to fight about. This one is par for the course.

JACK:       My daughter is three. Her mother and I have been divorced for a year, and I recently remarried. My daughter feels very comfortable calling my new wife Mommy when she visits with us. I think it's a good thing, because it means she has adjusted to the situation and feels comfortable with my remarriage. But my ex-wife, Kathy, is off the charts when it comes to this subject.

KATHY:    All I have to say is, how dare he? I have nothing against Jack's new wife, but she's not my daughter's mother, and she has a name. It's not Mommy. How would he like it if I

**They Call Her Mommy**

remarried and wanted our daughter to call my husband Daddy and use his surname? I bet you could hear him bellowing a thousand miles away.

## Judge Judy Says:

Jack, I'll make it easy for you. It seems to me that you want to keep as much peace as possible between yourself and Kathy, because Kathy is the primary custodian of your child. You're not doing it for Kathy's sake, you're doing it for your child's sake. And you don't want Kathy to be stressed every time your daughter comes back from visiting you, because her stress is going to have an impact on your daughter. Now, in all fairness to Kathy, she's got a point. Keep things simple. Your ex is Mommy, and your current wife is Jane. It's interesting to me how people get so tied up in knots about names and titles. The truth is, calling someone Mommy or Daddy doesn't necessarily mean that person is more cherished. I loved my father dearly, and he was in every way a great father. From the time I was a little girl, for some reason, I always called him by his first name. My brother called him Dad and I always called him Murry. Does that mean I loved him less? Not at all. The sun rose and set on my father, Murry.

# The Extra Grandma

Here's a different twist on the same theme.

JOYCE:  Gil and I have been married for twenty years.
We don't have children together, but Gil has
grown children from his first marriage. His
children and I developed a close, warm
relationship over the years, with the
understanding that their mother would always
still be number one for them. I not only
understood, I encouraged it; I wanted to be a
part of the family, not usurp their mother's
role. Well, Gil's daughter, Grace, got married a
few years ago, and just gave birth last year to a
gorgeous little girl. We're thrilled, of course,
and we visit frequently.

Now little Ellie is beginning to talk and
walk. Last week, I held out my arms to Ellie
and said, "Come to Grandma Joyce and give
her a big kiss!" Grace snapped at me. She
said, "Don't confuse Ellie. She has two
grandmothers—my mother, Lilly, and my
husband Bill's mother, Phyllis. Ellie can call
you Joyce." I was so insulted I left the house.
How dare she treat me this way? The awful
part is, Gil completely sides with his daughter,

and now he's furious with me for making a scene. I don't have any children of my own, and I was so looking forward to at least being a grandmother to this adorable little girl.

GIL:  I think my daughter, Grace, was unnecessarily hurtful to Joyce, and I told her so. She didn't mean to hurt Joyce's feelings, but she thinks it's too confusing for Ellie to have so many grandmothers. It's her choice, and we should accept it. Joyce is being overly sensitive.

## Judge Judy Says:

Names. Titles. Grandmother. Grandfather. Uncle, Dad, Mom. It gets complicated. I got married for a second time with my two little children in tow. My husband, Jerry, brought three of his own to the marriage. So we upped the ante first thing. I went from two kids to five; Jerry went from three kids to five. How'd we do? We managed just fine. Jerry's a great father. Did my kids call Jerry Daddy? No. They called him Jerry. His kids called him Dad. Did they call me Mom? No, they called me Judy. Today, my grandchildren have oodles of grandparents. A couple over here; a couple over there; a couple more over here and over there. Any problems? No. Why? Simple. Because there's plenty of love to go around. That's what it's all about: loving little children. Can little children have too many people loving them? I don't think so. They may get some of the titles confused. When my grandkids began to talk, they called me Nanna, and they called Jerry Poppy. They call my former husband Grandpa and his wife Grandma. Does any of this matter? Not at all. Not a bit. The important thing is that there's enough love for everyone. That's what's really important. Joyce, you have my sympathy, but get over it. Little Ellie isn't going to love you any less if she calls you Joyce than if she calls you Grandma Joyce. As my father Murry would say, "I don't care *what* you call me. Just *call* me."

# That's Chutzpah

Both mothers and fathers of divorce are equally responsible for the financial and emotional support of their first family. Let me repeat: Don't start a second family until you are prepared to take care of both.

CORA:  My ex-husband and I were divorced two years ago. The court ordered him to pay $100 a week in child support for our son. We were both working at similar jobs, and he thought it was fair. We have both remarried, and I just had a second child. I want to give my new baby the same nurturing I gave my first and not work for

two years. I told my ex that I would need another $100 a week in child support. He hit the
roof. Should I hire a lawyer?

HARRY:   My new wife and I would like to start a family
together. She has no children. When my ex-
wife had her baby, I was pleased that my son
would have a sibling. I have been faithful in
paying my child support and play an active role.
Increasing my child support would preclude my
wife and I from having a baby. I don't think it's
fair for my ex-wife to make this demand.

## Judge Judy Says:

I'm with you, Harry. When each of you remarried, you
understood your financial obligations. Each of you took
on other responsibilities fully cognizant of the preexisting
ones. Let me put it this way: Cora would surely object if
your second family made it impossible for you to pay the
$100 a week for the child support. Cora, dear, supporting
a child is the responsibility of two parents. If your new
baby means that more money is necessary in your home,
don't look to Harry to pick up the slack.

# Still "Married" to the In-Laws

A person who can turn off his or her emotions like a
faucet probably isn't worth having as a mate. When I

married Jerry, he already had a mother-in-law from his first marriage. He truly liked her. Over the years, I came to appreciate her, too. Gert is a special person and a positive force in the lives of her grandchildren. The point is, when you marry a person who has been married before, expect to expand your familial horizons.

TAYLOR: I enjoy a close relationship with my former mother- and father-in-law. Paige and I have been divorced for four years and have two children. I recently remarried. Paige has not. My present wife says that there's something unhealthy about wanting to spend time with, have dinner with, commiserate on the phone with former in-laws. I may have fallen out of love with Paige and her with me, but that doesn't mean I can turn off feelings for people who were my family for fifteen years. I love my in-laws. They were wonderful parents to me. We were married when we were quite young, and I think it's ludicrous for me to sever my relationship with them. You don't turn off emotions for the entire family when you divorce. Not if you're a good person.

SHIRLEY: When Taylor and I married I understood he had an ex-wife with whom he would have contact, but the whole extended family business is stupid. There aren't enough hours in the day or weeks in the year to keep in touch with all this ex-extended family.

## Judge Judy Says:

Taylor, I think that you have everything in perspective. Nowhere is it written that because you divorce one person you have to divorce the whole family. The fact that you maintain a lovely relationship with your former in-laws, who happen to be, by the way, the grandparents of your children, suggests to me that you're a unique and special person. And certainly if you are not making the call ritualistically every day to your in-laws, but want to have an occasional dinner or phone conversation, there should be no resistance in your home. It's something you should dig your heels in about because it seems to me that Shirley is probably trying to be a little too controlling. Shirley, it sounds as if you have a fine, caring guy. He is sensitive to relationships, which is probably one of the reasons you fell in love with him. His desire to keep in touch with his former in-laws should be no big deal. You may find that you like them, too, and that would be lovely for the kids.

# 8

# The Family Bond

### (Honor your parents.)

We've talked a lot about the unconditional love parents must have for their children. Now it's time to turn it around. Children, as they grow into adulthood, should learn to love their parents unconditionally. There comes a time when you have to be mature, accept your parents as they are, try to forgive them for any sins you perceive they've committed against you, and move ahead. Ask yourself: Do you want to spend your life on a couch telling a therapist how damaged you are, or do you want to get out there and try to function? What does it mean to love your parents unconditionally as they get older?

# Driving Dad

There is an inevitable reversal of roles that occurs as parents age. As a premature example of that, I remember vividly the day my father and ten-year-old brother came home from the corner store, my father laughingly telling my mother that he finally felt safe when he crossed the street. My father was about forty then. It seems that when they had reached the corner and were about to cross a busy street, my brother had reached up, taken my father by his arm, carefully looked both ways, then guided him across. From a very early age, my brother was trying to reverse roles. I preferred to wait as long as humanly possible.

JACKIE:   My dad should not be driving a car. He's eighty-five, his eyesight is poor, his hearing is weak, and his reflexes are shot. It's a miracle he hasn't been killed or killed others. I'd be happy to drive him wherever he wants to go, but he gets outraged when I even broach the subject. I'm ready to hide his keys or have his car towed away.

HAROLD:   I have always been a careful driver. There is not one accident on my record. Jackie thinks because I'm older and her mother is gone, she can boss me around. She doesn't have the right. If the Department of Motor Vehicles thought I was too old to drive, they'd take my license away.

## Judge Judy Says:

This is an emotional issue in many families. Jackie, you need to understand that driving a car represents your father's sense of freedom and independence. He doesn't want to be beholden to you whenever he wants to go out. Harold, you need to acknowledge that your daughter has a legitimate concern for your welfare. Maybe you could meet her halfway and limit your driving to the corner store or church. I recently met the ninety-six-year-old aunt of a colleague. She was terrific, and at ninety-six she still drives a car. She drives only during the day, always in the right-hand lane, and only for short distances. She clearly recognizes her limits. This lady is vital and independent, without being reckless.

# Too Old to Marry?

Sometimes adult children need to butt out of their parents' business.

MANDEL:  I am a seventy-two-year-old, healthy, vigorous man, and I've been alone for three years since my wife died. We were married for thirty-two years. I am financially secure and now retired. Last year, I was introduced to a terrific girl. Gloria also lost her husband several years ago. She is sixty-five and has two grown kids. She works part-time to supplement her Social Security. We have discussed getting married. Gloria would stop working, and we'd divide our time between New York and Florida, where I have homes. When I told my kids, all of a sudden they became more interested in my money than my happiness. They suggested that at our age we should not complicate our estates and just live together. God forbid I should have told them who and when to marry. Not that they made such great choices on their own, I might add. I think they should MYOB (Mind Your Own Business).

RACHEL:   Maybe we should have a committee appointed for our father. He's not thinking straight. We're glad he found somebody to have dinner with and go to an occasional movie with. We wouldn't even mind if they lived together, but the idea of their getting married and complicating the finances after he dies is ridiculous.

## Judge Judy Says:

Rachel, whose money is it, anyway? If your father wants to leave his money to the local humane society or a bird sanctuary, that's his prerogative. In this day and age, seventy-two years old is young. Your father may have ten or twenty years of life during which he can enjoy himself. If he wants to marry, that's his business. He doesn't tell you how to live your life. You don't have the right to tell him how he should live his.

# Never a Lender Be

Few things spark dissent in families like a loan that goes unpaid.

FRED:     I had some great business successes several
          years ago, and became so wealthy that I was
          able to retire when I was fifty-five. My wife,
          Beth, and I travel extensively for pleasure. We
          raised our sons to be responsible businessmen,
          and have always given them everything they've
          needed. They approached me a couple of years
          ago about starting their own business; they
          wanted me to extend them a substantial loan.
          Short-term, they said. Well, it's been over two
          years now. They started their business, and

they're still in business, but I haven't seen a dime. I finally asked them for my money point-blank, and they said they have no extra cash available to start paying the loan back. There is an important principle at stake here, and I've insisted on their paying back the loan immediately. This whole thing has blown up into a war, and my wife is furious with me.

BETH: I don't understand my husband at all. We have more money than we'll ever need, but he's stingy with our sons. The boys needed some help, he extended it, and now he's making out like he needs his stinking money back or he'll suffer.

## Judge Judy Says:

Beth, have you ever heard the phrase, "No good deed goes unpunished?" That seems to apply in this particular instance. Fred was asked to lend money, not give it. So he lent it with the clear expectation that he would have it returned to him. Your sons sound as if they need to learn a valuable lesson. Their father helped change their lives for the better, helped them to open their own business, and all of you are now angry with him. You're disappointed that he didn't suddenly decide to turn his loan into an outright gift. Maybe he would feel differently if your sons showed they had some integrity. The boys should start repaying the loan. Perhaps if they made this gesture, Fred would tell them to forget it, but it's his prerogative, not theirs.

# Taking Care of Mom

As the baby boomers grow older and their parents live longer, many people become their parents' caretakers.

STACEY:   I'm the baby of my family. I have three siblings, a brother and two sisters. We're all married and have our own families; we also all work, although I'm the only one of the four of us who works from her home. Our mom is going to be eighty soon, and until recently was as healthy as a horse. In the last year or so, she started having some health problems, and she needs a lot of medical care. We all live a good forty-five-minute drive from Mom's house. The first few times she had to get to the doctor, I was the one who took her there, because I can usually control my work schedule more easily than my siblings. Well, this has become a regular thing, and it's been very hard on me and my family. Also, it's expensive. I'm

spending a good twenty dollars more a week
for gas, and another ten dollars or so on tolls.
It adds up, never mind driving an extra three
or four hours every week. When I suggested to
my siblings that any of the three of them try to
help me out, you could have heard the
bleating and carrying on from the next county!
I resent the way they are behaving. All I'm
asking is that they help me. I can't handle this
all on my own.

TIM, MARGUERITE, AND TANYA: First of all, we all make an
effort to spend time with our mother every
week. It's only because Stacey has such
flexible work hours that she was elected to
take Mom to the doctor's office. None of us
can do it without taking scheduled, unpaid
time off from our jobs. Not all of us can have
the advantage of working at home; she does.
Stacey has the time to look after Mom, so it
falls on her to do it. We would if we could, but
we can't, so we don't. But Mom's doing all
right, and that's all that's important, isn't it?

## Judge Judy Says:

Life is no bed of roses, and it isn't always fair, either. I'm
sure that as children, some of you were more difficult

than the others, weren't you? Maybe one of you was sick a lot when you were little; your mother didn't give up on you because you were more work, did she? No. She treated you all with love and caring, according to your needs. Having said that, this is the time for all of you to make an effort, stretch the boundaries a little. Stacey isn't an only child. So I have a couple of suggestions. First, all of you have to make some sacrifices for your mom. Not necessarily on an equal basis, but there are ways each of you can chip in. That means taking your mom to doctor's appointments; that also means giving Stacey some cash to help defray her transportation expenses. Maybe your mom could pitch in and help with the expenses. If she's financially capable, you should ask her. Lastly, be grateful that you still have your mom in your lives, and let her know that you love her, care about her, and don't view her as a chore. The way to do that is very practical: You show up at her door and take her to the doctor's office. You wait for her. On the way home, maybe you take her food shopping, or maybe you've made something to eat, and you bring it to her house so you'll know she has food and is eating well. Take care of your mother; she took care of you once. It's her turn now.

# Honor Your Parents

The best way to honor your parents is to accept them and love them as they really are, not as you wish they would be. By the time people are in their fifties, sixties, and beyond, they're fully formed human beings. They're not going to suddenly become different because their children push them. I had a case in my television courtroom that was a superb example. A solid older couple, originally from Central Europe, were suing for emotional distress they said was inflicted during a "therapeutic" weekend getaway their son had arranged for them. He wanted his parents to become, as he put it, "more in touch with their feelings." He wanted to break through their Old World reserve and turn them into touchy-feely types. In other words, "change." Good parents accept their children for who they are. When they don't, the children are usually angry—for good reason. It works both ways.

NILDA:    I'm getting married next September. I met the love of my life, Sam, last year, just after I turned forty. Sam is five years older than I am, and he's never been married before either. Sam's great, and we love each other very much. We met at our jobs—we're both real estate lawyers. My problem is with my parents. Next month, Sam and I are going to host a dinner to bring our parents together for the first time. Sam's parents are educated people. They're very cultured and sophisticated. My parents are wonderful people, but they're not formally educated. I've asked my parents to buy some special clothes for the evening (I know their wardrobe). I even offered to take them shopping. They became very angry, and said that if I was ashamed of them, we could just skip the dinner. I'm not ashamed of them. I just want them to look their best, so they can put their best foot forward when they meet Sam's parents.

MIKE (Nilda's father): After all the sacrifices we've made for Nilda over the years, this just kills her mother and me. Now she makes us feel like we're not good enough for her new family, that we're not good enough to meet her guy's parents. Suddenly we're second-class citizens. Our clothes were good enough for her college graduation. If she's afraid we'll embarrass her, we'll just stay home.

## Judge Judy Says:

Nilda, the moment for a heartfelt apology to your parents has arrived. I find you guilty of being insensitive and a bit shallow. Let me tell you something about Sam's parents: If they care even one iota about what your parents are wearing, I'll eat my hat.

# The Baby and the Grandparents

A lot of energy gets expended in families trying not to cause any hurt feelings. Meanwhile, resentments are quietly flourishing. You can be honest and also be gentle.

LARRY:    Jill and I just had our first baby, a little girl we named Molly. Jill's parents, Stuart and Phyllis, are wonderful, wonderful people, and we've always had a good relationship. Since the baby came, they've practically moved in with us. They're at our house every day, and that includes the weekends. Jill and Molly and I almost never have a moment alone, and it's starting to get to me. When I told Jill how I felt, we had a huge argument. She finally admitted that she'd like a break from her folks, too, but she doesn't know how to tell them without hurting their feelings. Jill says that eventually the novelty of the baby will wear off, and they'll show up less often. I'm not so sure that's true.

JILL: How can he expect me to tell my parents that they're not welcome in our home? They've been great. They can't do enough to help. They're just gaga over their first grandchild, that's all.

## Judge Judy Says:

I remember when my first grandchild was born. I wanted to be there every day. Fortunately for my daughter, I worked. There has to be a balance, and it never has to reach the point where there's a big showdown at the O.K. Corral. Jill, tell your folks that you've made plans with some friends next weekend, and set a time to see them on Monday. Keep repeating this scenario for a couple of weeks, and the "drop-in" habit will begin to be modified. There's no need for a head-on confrontation. Just be smart.

# Maid Service

When Jerry and I first had our house on the lake, our kids and grandkids loved to come up for the weekends. They had a great time boating, swimming, biking, and playing ball. Jerry was the entertainment director—a role at which he has always excelled. That left me with housekeeping.

Was I resentful? You bet. Did I suffer in silence? You know me better than that.

IRENE:   Irving and I have been married for a year. We're both in our sixties and we live in a nice little community in Florida, near the beach. This is my third marriage and Irving's second. Irving's grown daughter, Sheila, and her two teenage girls come to visit and stay with us twice a year, for two weeks at a time. They're all very close to Irving, very loving, which of course I approve of. My problem is a simple one: They're all complete slobs, and I spend their entire visit cleaning up after them, doing laundry, shopping, and cooking meals. For Irving alone, I don't mind doing it. But for his daughter and her two teenagers, it's frankly a lot of work. While Irving and the girls are bonding, I'm working like a maid for them.

IRVING:   I get to see my daughter and her girls only twice a year. I want the visits to be like a vacation for them. Is it really such a big deal if Irene has to expend a little extra effort for a couple of weeks?

## Judge Judy Says:

Irving, in a word: Yes. It's too much to ask of Irene. If you don't want your daughter or your granddaughters to have to lift a finger, you should help out yourself. Better still, arrange to have someone come in and help—hire a housekeeper for the laundry and general cleaning up. You can also take your family out to eat, so Irene won't have to cook. Perhaps you would prefer to put your family up in a nice motel nearby where they have maid service. Irene, you have a right to not suffer in silence. Two visits a year adds up to four weeks a year. It should be a pleasure for all of you.

# Social Insecurity

What good are the "golden years" if you can't enjoy them? That's what Sarah wondered, too.

SARAH:    Harry and I are both in our seventies, and
          after dating for six months, we decided to live
          together. He sublet his small apartment and
          moved into mine, which is bigger and much
          nicer. We both get Social Security, and I have
          some savings—so did Harry. I found out before
          he moved in with me that he turned over most
          of his money to his daughter. When I asked

him what about us, he said, "I can get by on my Social Security. If you need more for vacations or eating out, you should take it out of your savings." I'm furious about this, and I told him he should get his money back. Why should he give up control of his money to his daughter now, and put us in a position where we're pinching every penny?

HARRY:    I didn't think Irene was interested in my money. I thought she wanted me for the sex–ha-ha. For years I hardly touched my savings, and I saw no need to when we moved in together. It was smart estate planning to give gifts to my daughter and her children.

## Judge Judy Says:

Parents should never give their children all of their money. That places you at their mercy in case of an emergency. So my advice to you, Harry, is to be generous, but not stupid. Estate planning is smart, but leaving yourself virtually penniless isn't smart; it's dumb. Harry, get your money back—if you can!

## 9

# 'Til Death Do Us In

### (Where there's a will, there's a way.)

Dying creates so many problems that I wish we could all just forget about it. Since none of us can choose dancing over dying, plan we must. Those who don't plan often leave a trail of fighting, frustration, and litigation. There might be fighting in any event, but at least with a will you have done your part in disposing of your assets, not to mention yourself.

## The Plot Thickens

Remarriage not only complicates life, but it can complicate the afterlife as well—as this family learned when the subject of plots came up.

**The Plot Thickens**

YOLANDA: My parents were married for forty-one years before Mom died. My father remarried and has been married to Micheline for eight years. Now he is quite ill. Dad is very organized and is making plans for his final resting place. There is a plot that is right next to my mother. Micheline insists that they buy two plots and that they be buried together. Her first husband is still alive, and judging from the stories of their divorce, I doubt that they'd be buried together. But I think Dad should be buried next to Mom, where he belongs.

MICHELINE: While this is a very sad time for us, the last eight years that Wayne and I have spent together have been joyous and fulfilling. We really found soulmates in each other. I honestly believe that we should be buried together so that I will not be alone. If Wayne's children don't want their mother to be alone, they can use one of the plots that's reserved for them when they die. But I want to be with Wayne. We belong together.

## Judge Judy Says:

It sounds to me as if everyone is making poor old Dad's final days even more difficult. He's the one who's ill. He's the one who's contemplating death. Let him enjoy his remaining time without the noise of your bickering. The choice of where one lives is theirs. And the choice of a final resting place should also be theirs. This is Dad's decision, and his alone.

From a strictly legal perspective, should he die without having made these arrangements, it would be Micheline's decision, as his surviving spouse, about where he would be buried. That's the way the law views it. But since Dad is trying to make these plans, let him make them in peace. Yolanda, if you and your siblings have to make two trips to two different locations to visit your parents' graves, would it really be such an imposition? They were good to you in life; be good to them in death.

# Stop Your Squawking

When a parent dies, it is usually a very emotional period for the adult children. Too often they transfer those emotions into bickering over money and possessions.

PHYLLIS:   My father died recently, leaving everything to my sister and me. Here's the problem. Dad had a rare, very expensive parrot. I hate the bird, my sister loves it, and she can have it. But this bird is worth at least $10,000, and I think she should pay me half of the value.

EMILY:    I think that's sick. Petey is like a member of the family, not a possession. My sister would sell her own children to make a buck.

## Judge Judy Says:

Sisters! Stop making Dad roll over in his grave. If parents understood what their lack of planning could do their children, they would die penniless or run to the nearest estate planner. The bird belongs to Pat. This is what Dad would want. If total financial fairness is what you require, choose something of equal value of his and keep it. If not, be content in knowing that Dad is happy that his pet is well cared for.

# Where There's a Will

Janet and Carl have been married their entire adult lives, have raised two children, and are in every sense a partnership. You'd think that the matter of wills would be pretty simple at this point. Not so.

JANET:    My husband and I have been married for thirty-five years and his business has been very successful. We're in the process of preparing our wills, and my husband has decided that in addition to leaving a substantial portion of the estate to me and to our children, he wants to leave bequests to his two siblings. I have no objection to that, but I also have a sibling and if he's going to leave money to his two brothers, he should leave money to my sister. He always said our money was our money. Now he says if he dies he wants to be able to bequeath his money the way he believes it's appropriate. I always thought it was a partnership.

CARL:    I don't see the problem. I'm leaving three-quarters of my fortune to my wife if I die first. If she wishes to bequeath any part of that to her sister in her will, she's free to do that.

## Judge Judy Says:

What are the issues here? Carl is concerned about making sure that should he die first, his siblings will receive some portion of his money. Janet has the same concerns about her sister. The solution seems to be obvious: You can each make provisions in your respective wills that take care of your respective siblings in the event of your death. Carl can add a provision that should Janet predecease him, on his death her sister would receive benefits. There. All the bases are covered.

# Prenuptial Nudging

Richard's children have been very protective of their father since their mother's death ten years ago. Now that he's planning to remarry, they're having a heated debate about Dad's money.

RICHARD: I am sixty-two, and was married for twenty-five years before my wife died. We have three wonderful children. I've been financially successful and have provided for my children all during their lives. I am planning to marry a woman who's fifty-five, and also a widow. My children insist that I enter into a prenuptial agreement because I have a substantial estate and she has very little money. I think it would be hurtful to start this new relationship with a prenuptial agreement. At my age, I don't feel old. How would my kids react if I told them how to dispose of the substantial moneys I've given them over the years? I might add that none of them have prenuptial agreements and most of their assets were gifts from me. I will continue to provide for my children and give them a gift during my lifetime, but I think it's

wrong for them to insist that they have any say
whatsoever in how I use my money.

SAMANTHA: I'm glad that my dad has found somebody,
but that doesn't mean he has to be a fool. We
are his children. There is no question that he's
more than generous to us, but don't we have
any say in what happens to this family money?

## Judge Judy Says:

I've always felt that when two people are in love, it's difficult to raise the issue of a prenuptial agreement before
you walk down the aisle. But Richard, there are very easy
ways to ensure that your wife will be taken care of financially should something happen to you. May I suggest
that you consult an attorney who specializes in estates?
There are ways to ensure that your wife, should you predecease her, will have the income from your assets, and
that upon her death the money will go to your children. If
there is an afterlife, you will feel like a fool if after your
wife's death your hard-earned money went to strangers
instead of your own children. A prenuptial agreement
doesn't have to be a sour note. I'll bet your wife-to-be
would feel very good about your saying, "I want to ensure
that you are comfortable upon my death, so that you will
have the vast majority of the income from my resources

while you're alive. And after that the money goes to my children and my grandchildren." That is a reasonable solution.

# Inheriting the Wind

You'd be surprised at the hurricane-level emotion that gets kicked up about inheritances. It isn't so much that children are greedy. It's a more complex mix of emotion and money. Children, irrespective of their age, like to feel as if their parents love them equally. How do you say "I love you" to an adult child? You treat them the same. You try to give to them equally. Right or wrong, they will see any disparity as a sign of their relative worth in your eyes. Now, if you believe that one of your children doesn't need the money as much as another child, you have to get it out in the open and discuss it with the less needy child. Say, "How would you feel if I left more to your sister because she really needs it?" Some people would say, "Fine, I don't care." Others would say, "I think you should treat us equally."

MIRIAM:   I'm preparing my will. My son John is a hard
          worker. He works twelve hours a day. He's a
          good father. He has been financially success-

ful. My other son, Alan, has always needed a
little bit of help. He and his wife struggle to
get by. Alan has trouble holding down a job,
and I feel some responsibility to see that he
and his family are secure, that Alan's children
will be able to go to college and have the same
advantages as their uncle's children. When I
explained to John that I felt it was right for me
to leave Alan a larger portion of the estate, he
was very offended. At the moment, we're not
even speaking. I don't know how to resolve
this.

JOHN:     Why should I be punished for being a hard
worker? That's what this is all about. I hope
my mother lives to be 120, but I always
thought that eventually I wouldn't have to
worry about my retirement because there
would be that little nest egg that came to me
through my mother from my father. But here
she is pulling that out from under me because
my brother needs daily support. It's not fair.

## Judge Judy Says:

Miriam, John is absolutely right. He *is* being penalized for
being a hard worker. While I understand that you want to
provide for your grandchildren, that can be accomplished

during your lifetime. To ensure that each of your grand-children has a little bit of money, set up trust funds for them now so they will at least have a jump start on college. In your will, treat both sons equally. Otherwise you will create an estrangement between them that will continue long after you are gone.

# 10

# Keep It Simple, Stupid

## (You're smarter than you look.)

Life is a one-shot deal. There are only so many seconds, minutes, hours, days, and years. Every second you devote to negative energy and negative emotion is a second lost forever. What if you were told you had only a week to live? Would you spend that week getting your revenge on those who you think wronged you? Would your thoughts be of retribution? Not if you were normal. Revenge would be the last thing on your mind. Grudges would seem insignificant. You'd want to get all of your affairs in order, and be surrounded by those you loved, and who loved you. What I've tried to suggest through these stories is that we unnecessarily complicate our daily lives. We create circumstances that gobble up precious time—our time. We needlessly involve ourselves in trivial issues that in the big picture don't mean squat:

Who cares if the wedding invitation includes all the names in Genesis, as long as the bride and groom are happy?

Who cares if Dad is buried in Plot A or Plot B, as long as he enjoyed himself while he was alive?

Who cares if your ex gets the upper hand once in a while, as long as your kids are happy and secure?

Who cares if your grandkids call you Grandma, Nanna, or Sue–as long as they call you?

What I'm proposing is simply this: Sit down, take a deep breath, and target the ultimate objective in every situation.

If you're beginning a new relationship, your objective is to get to know each other, to find out if this is the "one." Keep things unentangled until you move from learning to commitment. Don't rush into opening joint anythings— leases, bank accounts, property, or credit cards. Nothing.

If you're planning a wedding, the ultimate objective should be that the bride and groom have a memorable and meaningful day—the perfect beginning to their married lives together. Anything that detracts from that objective should not be an issue. If Aunt Sally is miffed because she's seated too close to the band, she'll have to deal with it. It's not your problem.

Your objective as a married couple is to love and support one another as partners through good times and bad. "Until death" can be a long time if you're obsessing over every wrongly squeezed toothpaste tube or every visit to the in-laws. You can choose to be happily married or you can choose to be miserably married.

Even when divorce is imminent, stay focused on the objective–to leave with dignity, to shelter your children from distress, to be free of anger and resentment.

Families and relationships are complicated; they can be maddening. Surprises are inevitable–and they're not always going to be happy surprises. It's the tradeoff for being involved with other people, and most of us agree that the tradeoff is worth it. If you stay focused on what really matters, you'll avoid a lot of irritation. Do the simple things: Organize yourself as much as you can. Return calls promptly, pay your bills on time, and keep a list of family birthdays and anniversaries. Plan ahead, and control those areas that are within your power. Because when the unexpected occurs–and it always does—you'll be better able to cope. Keeping it simple is just a matter of eliminating all the excess baggage so you can enjoy a happier life. Trust me, you can do it. You're smarter than you look.